LAW OF ATTRACTION

YOUR SECRET TO ATTRACT MONEY, LOVE, SUCCESS, AND HAPPINESS IN YOUR LIFE NOW

ZACHARIAH ALBERT

CONTENTS

INTRODUCTION

Looking closely at our everyday life, you will realize that the law of attraction is present all the time. Most people do not notice the connection because of the time lag between their thoughts and the manifestation of their thoughts. However, there are some things that happen to us that we feel happened as a result of a coincidence, not knowing it is the law of attraction that is at work. For instance, have you ever thought of calling a friend, and the friend calls you around that time? Or have you ever thought of picking up your phone, and your phone rings at that instance? These experiences are not coincidences; they are a result of the law of attraction.

We get more of what we focus on in life. That is why you need to get more creative with your thoughts.

In this book, I am going to show you how you can consciously and deliberately attract good things into your life by aligning your thoughts in the right way.

Focusing more on things that make you happy increases your chances of attracting things that make you happy. The other side of this is the negative side which is when you focus on things you are not happy about, you tend to attract things that will make you sad. For instance, if you focus on wealth and good health, you attract wealth and good health. However, if you focus on poverty, you will attract a situation that will rob you of the little things you have gathered.

This is the premise on which the law of attraction is built. You get more of what you focus on. This is one of the reasons thinking negatively can be very harmful to your life. Being in a constant state of worry about the past, present, or likely occurrence of events in the future can trigger one of the most powerful laws in the universe to work against you because you are attracting the things you do not want. You can use the law of attraction to attract a lot of good things in your life.

1. **Love:** The law of attraction lets you know that you can't give out one thing and receive another. Being guided by the law of

attraction will first help you to love yourself before loving another person. If you desire genuine and sweet love, you learn to give yourself that genuine and sweet love, and then, a person that can give you what you desire will become attracted to you. The law of attraction helps you work on yourself all round and prepares you to receive love and give it out also.

2. **Money:** As much as we all love money and want to be financially stable, we know that money also has its negative parts like greed, pride, and so on. We want money, but we keep thinking of how difficult it is to get or the fear of the money bring stolen when gotten. The law of attraction teaches that you can't give out negativity to get positivity. Harboring these negative thoughts about money will definitely attract them to you. Learn to adopt positive practices towards money, and money will become abundant around you. Remind yourself that you are not a slave to money. Instead, money works for you. Money is vital, but don't exalt it too much that you become a slave to it.

3. **Happiness:** The law of attraction helps us see the best in everything and sometimes when we get carried away with our responsibilities and things that we haven't done, we become upset. There will always be things yet to be done, but you shouldn't beat yourself up about them. Keep seeing the positive side of everything, and you will end up being happy all the time. When you keep expecting the best out of any situation, the best will come to you. Also, when we are happy, it benefits our mental and physical health.

You do not need to go through a special routine to activate the law of attraction. The law is always at work because you are always thinking. The only thing you have to do is make a conscious decision to control your thoughts and use the law to your advantage.

Most people in this generation judge their reality by their senses – what they see, taste, touch, hear and smell. They judge things by the way they appear. They make a careful observation of their environment, and channel their thoughts to be similar to it. Even the Bible advises us against it in the book of John chapter 7, verse 24. "Do not judge by external standards." You have to fully enter into a mental state where you mirror the things you want, not a state where you constantly focus on not having what you want.

Visualize how you will like your life to be. Always carry this image in mind, and create a lot of positive emotion around it. This will put the law of attraction into effect in your life, and then, you will start to see the manifestation of that vision you have created in your mind.

To get the things you desire speedily and activate this law in your life, you need to have the ability to visualize the things you want. You need to have clarity about what you want to create. Even though this is common sense, it is still very surprising that most people do not have an idea of what they want. They have no problem telling you what they do not want, but when it comes to what they want, they are lost for words. They are unclear about their desires. They want riches but do not know how much riches they want. They crave for a different career, but cannot seem to decide which is best for them. They want better rapport with their partner, family, or friends, but do not know what it is supposed to look like or feel like. You have to refrain from vague thinking if you want to live life your own way.

Reflect on a part of your life where you feel something seems to be lacking or could be better, an area where you feel if improved, you will feel happier and much better.

Have a clear focus on what you will like to happen. Will you like to have a better relationship with your family and friends? Or would you want to have a new career? Would you like to improve on your health and fitness level? Just be specific and choose an area.

Now that you have decided on that area, you need to decide the result you would like to see in that particular area. Be extremely sure of what you want in that area. If you will like to have a new career, what kind of career will you like to have? Or, if it is a better relationship you will like to have, what type of partner will you like to have? What characteristics and traits will you like your partner to have? What values will you like him or her to have? Do you want your finances to be better? Would you prefer to have just enough, or will you prefer to have a huge sum of money? Be detailed about it.

Now, pen it down. Write in form of an affirmation. Let it be written in such a way that a stranger will understand how you want your life to be just by reading it. Write it like you are explaining your life to yourself. Read this written affirmation out loud to yourself every morning and night, and visualize it like it's existing already. Create positive emotions around the affirmations. Emotions help to activate the law of attraction. Thoughts can be imaginative, but emotions fuel the thoughts into manifestation.

Go on with your daily activities, and focus on your outlined goals. If a negative thought pops in your mind for a short while, pause for a moment, and change the thoughts to positive. Meditate on it until the only emotion you feel about it is positive.

Open yourself to opportunities. If you diligently follow your daily visualizations, you will notice that more doors of opportunity will be open to you.

Take action! Act towards your goals no matter how small the action might seem. Search for new jobs, meet more people, and find out ways you can improve your finances. The universe will meet you halfway when you take steps towards your goal.

CHAPTER 1
A BRIEF HISTORY OF THE LAW OF ATTRACTION

I have heard a lot of people talk about the power of the law of attraction. I have heard about the principles of "like energies can only attract like energies." I did research about it and realized that the law of attraction is one of the many laws that rule the universe. There are so many laws that rule the universe. Some of them are The 12 immutable Universal laws, the spiritual laws, and the Universal laws of Nature. These laws might not be called the same names, and some of them have specific instructions attached to them, but at the end of the day, you will find out that the laws are very similar to each other.

The first and most important principle is: physical reality is a projection from an interconnected conscious-

ness, which has infinite potential. To put it a different way, physical reality is energy vibrating at different frequencies that our minds perceive as matter. This energetic field, if you will, comes from pure consciousness– which all religions would refer to as God. The other laws expand on this stating that everything is energy; your thoughts, emotions, and even actions are energy that affects other energy. Therefore, what you decide to focus on will attract other energies that are vibrating at the same frequency. [1] - This is the main idea behind most of the laws that rule the universe.

The law of attraction did not just begin in this new generation; it dates way back to the olden days, far from the belief that it's a new generation phenomenon.

Buddha was one of the first people to introduce man to the law of attraction, as he said, "what you become is what you think." Karma also draws its roots from the law of attraction as karma states that, "what goes around comes around," meaning if you have offended another one way or the other, you will, in turn, be visited with the same cruelty you've meted out on another, but if you've been kind to another, then you'll be visited with the same kindness.

It is not farfetched that the revival of the law of attraction is associated with the happiness of the world. The law of attraction was absent in the Dark and Middle Ages. It is common knowledge that the Dark Age was not a very good time to be alive. The revival period was a rebirth of arts, writing, and knowledge. It was because the law of attraction and the teachings of Hermes resurfaced around that time. The law of attraction made a huge comeback in the 1800s. It caused a great industrial revolution at the time, and the drive is still very much present till now. There is no data to back this up, but when you study and observe American history, you will observe this.

The interesting part of world history is not what we see now with the technology and new knowledge but the events of thousands of years ago. The Egyptian leaders were strong believers of the law of attraction, and they achieved great things at the time, and some of the things that were achieved are being replicated now. The Greeks and Romans also made a great impact on the paths of learning, philosophy, arts, and science, but when the law of attraction was less practiced, the discoveries diminished.

The law of attraction was not limited to Egyptians only. It was also practiced by Muslims, Christians, and Babylonians because it is part of their teachings. The eastern culture also practiced these laws, and it was evident in their healing techniques. The fact, that sometimes when one person in an elderly couple dies, the partner also dies after a short while, shows that our mind, thoughts, and the physical body are connected. Most times, those who are constantly afraid of falling sick tend to fall sick eventually. This points to the fact that we can learn a lot about happiness and success from history.

THE HERMETIC PRINCIPLES

The spiritual laws that rule the universe were listed in The Seven Hermetic Principles by the wise and mystical man called Hermes Trismegistus. These laws were later transliterated in The Emerald Tablet of Hermes and in The Kybalion.

. These principles are as follows (these are Hermes' interpretation of the laws according to the authors of The Kybalion):

1. **The Principle of Mentalism:** "THE ALL IS MIND; the Universe is Mental." When Hermes said, "The ALL", he meant the force that manifests the physical Universe (what we would call God today). If this

doesn't sound like the first principle of the newer Universal Laws, it should, because they are one and the same.

2. **The Principle of Correspondence:** "As above, so below; as below, so above." Hermes believed there were multiple planes/realms of the material, mental, and spiritual universe, and that there is always a correspondence between the laws and phenomena of the various planes of being. This means the laws that govern the higher spiritual realm also govern the lower material realms. This law is called the same thing in the new 12 Immutable Universal Laws.

3. **The Principle of Vibration:** "Nothing rests; everything moves; everything vibrates." This states everything that makes up the Universe from Matter, Energy, Mind, and Spirit, is manifested through different levels of vibration. This is one of the Laws that has continuously been proven with modern sciences like Quantum Physics, which I will focus more on in the next chapters.

4. **The Principle of Polarity:** "Everything is Dual; everything has poles; everything has its pair of opposites; like and unlike are the same; opposites are identical in nature, but different in degree; extremes met; all truths are but half-truths; all paradoxes may be reconciled." This is the yin and yang of the eastern religions. Everything in the Universe, including thought, has its polar opposite. This principle is not only found in the eastern philosophies/religions but is being proven true with Quantum Physics as well.

5. **The Principle of Rhythm:** "Everything flows, out and in; everything has its tides; all things rise and fall; the pendulum-swing manifests in everything; the measure of the swing to the right is the measure of the swing to the left; rhythm compensates." This incorporates the principles of vibration, polarity, and even the not yet mentioned 'cause and effect' to show there is a rhythm in everything in the Universe, and everything goes through cycles.

6. **The Principle of Cause and Effect:** "Every Cause has its Effect; every Effect has its Cause; everything happens according to Law; Chance is but a name for Law not recognized; there are many planes of causation, but nothing escapes the Law." If you want to track where the Law of Attraction originated, you found it. It states that nothing ever happens by chance. If something happens to you, you manifested it. If something happens to us as a whole, we manifested it.

7. **The Principle of Gender:** "Gender is in everything; everything has its Masculine and Feminine Principles; Gender manifests on all planes." This principle states that gender (masculine and feminine energies) are manifested in all planes of existence. In the physical plane, it is manifested through the male and female sexes. In the higher planes of existence, this is manifested in different ways, but the principle applies there as well (if it didn't it would break the 2nd principle).[2]

This is a very simple look at the valuable teaching

of Hermes Trismegistus. He was a highly intelligent man and a very deep philosopher who had discovered things about the universe that science just started exploring.

This is not the only place that these principles have been found to work. These principles have been found in the teachings of others from ancient days.

The first Hermetic principle which is the idea that the mind is everything is found in Buddha's teachings which say, "All that we are is the result of what we have thought. The mind is everything. What we think, we become."

However, Buddhism is not the only religion that has quotes similar to the Hermetic Spiritual Principles. These principles are also found in multiple places in the bible. In Matthew 7:7-9, Jesus said, "Ask, and it will be given to you; seek, and you will find; knock, and it will be opened to you. (8) For everyone who asks, receives, and he who seeks finds, and to him who knocks, it will be opened. (9) Or what man is there among you who when his son asks for a loaf will give him a stone?" In Mark 11:24, He also said, "Therefore, I say to you, all things for which you pray and ask, believe that you have received them, and they will be granted you." These biblical quotes spoken by Jesus focus on the law of attraction and the other Hermetic

Laws. The last sentence of the above quote states clearly that God, the creator of the universe, will not hand you anything different from what you put your focus on.

The law of attraction was made more popular by the book and documentary "The secret". The book claims that the law has been in practice for centuries by a few people who used it and kept it hidden from the rest of the world. The teachings of the law were very popular in ancient times, and they were taught by people like Plato.

However, during the years, the knowledge somehow stopped being passed down to other generations except in Occults like Alchemist and Mystics. Lately, Quantum Physics has been proving a lot of Hermetic principles to be accurate. However, there has been propaganda against the laws of attraction by the mainstream media and mainstream scientific establishments. There is a possibility that this is happening because people do not know that they are in complete control of their destiny. However, if more people are aware that they are in complete control of their destiny, they won't be easily controlled by the media.

If you are still doubtful of the power of the law of attraction, then I will encourage to do a little test. Try to control your thoughts, actions, and emotions.

Anytime you notice yourself thinking negatively or start acting fearful, be immediately conscious about it, stop the thought, and start thinking about positive effects. After sometimes, you will begin to experience some changes in you and your environment. When you do this and see results, you will see that Hermes was right when he said you could create your destiny, no matter the people who tell you that you cannot.

Some very interesting ideas similar to the law of attraction are described in the Hermetica. Some of the basic ideas are:

1. Everything has energy, and everything is always changing (turns out to be true).
2. The universe is full of energy that people can connect to and gain power from (law of attraction).
3. There is no good or bad. There is a balance in the world of worse or better. Something good to someone may be bad to another. Something that appears bad at first may turn out to be good later on.
4. The goal of the highly-aware person is to stop themselves from feeling bad. The aware person can stop from sliding too far down the scale of feelings. They are aware

that things that seem bad may not be
so (huge law of attraction reference).

5. Most people naturally sway from feeling
good to feeling bad, but the key is to keep
yourself feeling good all the time to reach a
higher awareness. It also takes a lot
of focus, which is also a key to Hermes'
philosophies as well.[3]

Where are the Hermetic teachings today?

A lot of people still believe and practice the
hermetic teachings to date. There have been many
revivals of the hermetic teachings over the years. The
revival period experienced a huge revival about the
teachings. This revival which started in the mid-1800s
continued into the 20th century. There were huge gaps
between the dark ages and the middle ages when it
comes to the teachings. Some people speculated that
this gap was created so as to give way to a new way of
thinking- Christianity. Others speculated that The
Romans destroyed the information when Caesar burnt
the library of Alexander. There are also speculations
that the Muslims destroyed the information in the
sixth century.

The revivals of the Hermetic teachings and the law
of attraction were credited to the discovery of some

antique scrolls that survived over the years. The Revival period discovered tablets they believed were from ancient Egyptians. The scrolls that were discovered in the Dead Sea caused a rebirth from the information that was in them.

CHAPTER 2

THE SCIENCE OF LAW OF ATTRACTION

T he science of the law of attraction appeals to a wide range of disciplines which support the principles that people believe in. There is a scientific belief for positive thinking and its effect in the law of attraction. The law of attraction is also the law of nature which every atom in your body responds to. The effectiveness of the science of the law of attraction traces its roots back to physics and its other supporting facts like quantum mechanics.

The law of attraction is the most attractive and captivating power that draws corresponding energies together, and this can be revealed in many ways and through the power of creation. It attracts people with like minds, ideas, situations, and thoughts. It is this attraction that brings like-minded people together who unite to create different groups like the fraternities, the political clubs, and social clubs etc.

You can take advantage of the law of attraction to achieve whatever you want to achieve, by creating an image of what you want mentally or repeating positive statements of that which you wish to achieve. And if you think the law of attraction doesn't work for you, then try using science to make it happen because science proves that the law of attraction really works.

The science of the law of attraction can be found in neuroscience, biology, and quantum physics which might not be easy to understand at first because studying the science of the law of attraction might just be like studying science itself in a way you've never seen before. The science of the law of attraction consists of different aspects of life like being able to imagine your success, fixing your emotions, and the things you desire to have.

The law of attraction started becoming popular in the 19th century as people began to appreciate the power of positivity and applying it to their daily lives. The law of attraction actually works for everyone, and it has certain laws that govern it like The law of manifestation which implies that you have a choice to choose your state of consciousness, a choice to bring your awareness into your present moment, and decide to see and put first that which you consider as important and genuine to add value to your life.

The law of magnetism which implies that we attract the same kind of energy that we put out in ourselves. The World is filled with the vibration of energy which moves from within us and all around us all the time.

The law of desire which states that for you to be able to achieve that which you desire, you must first believe that you're truly worthy of that which you desire, and be happy about it.

The law of harmony which states that when you choose to create a balance consciously and fix yourself with the universe, your intentions and energy will open a gateway of abundance, allowing you access to enjoy all the wealth and blessings the universe has to offer you.

The law of right action which states that your actions should be able to promote your good values and dignity in your environment, but if your actions are wrong, then it will destroy your values in your environment.

These laws are the main ingredients that make up the law of attraction.

SCIENCE AND THE LAW OF ATTRACTION

Having beliefs that restrict you should not make you feel guilty. However, what you need to do now is to try to recognize these thoughts and make an effort to change them. Innovative genetic research has given a reason why you shouldn't fault yourself for the limiting beliefs that have the ability to stop you from effective manifestation.

Some specific scientists in Atlanta have established that when mice connected the cherry blossom to an electric shock, they become so scared of the scent that they eventually pass on the fear of it to their progeny through the genetic code. What this means is that even the mice that did not experience the shock will end up being afraid of the scent. Brain-imaging studies have also shown that this fear is characterized by the existence of altered neurological receptors. Even though you have negative beliefs holding you back, it is not entirely your fault. However, you have the ability to overcome these thoughts.

Different fields in academics are becoming more aware of the concepts that underline the law of attraction, and they are becoming more interested in researching more neurological evidence to back the claim that we have the ability to bring what we want in life into existence. If you take a look at latest research in biology, psychology, genetics, and neuro-science, it is certain you will find out more scientific law of attraction facts that shows that working with the law of attraction is very effective.

An integral part of the law of attraction is knowing how to be a straightforward, happy person who sends high-frequency vibration to people around you and produce a positive response in others. The manner in which radiate good attitudes toward everyone around us and attract kindness, liberality, and victory can somewhat be explained with reference to mirror neurons (neurons that "mirror" the behaviors we perceive).

This means that when someone sees you exhibiting positivity, the same positive response is reflected in the brain of the person observing it. This can make them show positive acts towards you. Also, studies of the brain's emotional center (amygdala) have shown that we have the ability to induce feelings of fear and anxiety in other people if we are showing fearfulness or anxiety.

This further explains the law of attraction theorist's claim that negative thinking can hinder success, happiness, love, and connection with other people.

Studies that were published recently show that

affirming positive things can help people heal from traumatic events, improve depressive symptoms, and is even generally related to having good well-being.

How the science of the law of attraction works?

According to Joellyn Wiitensten Schwerdlin, the law of attraction has five basic principles that help you understand how the law really works, and how it can be used to achieve results.

1. ***Principle 1: Understand sympathetic vibrations- this simply means that like attracts like.*** Like musical notes that vibrate, everything in the universe vibrates. As humans, we also vibrate and act out our feelings. Our feelings are fueled by our thoughts. When we think about good things we feel so good but when we think of something bad or even remember a bad event, we feel bad immediately. Those feelings are like vibrations that attract the same wavelength. If you want to work on your moods and feelings, then start from your thoughts.

2. ***Principle 2: Raise your vibrations*** – raise your feeling when you are feeling good. There are just two types of feelings, and they are good and bad. The law of attraction responds to your negative emotions, and that is the low vibration by bringing your way more negative situations. But when you choose to feel good, that is the high vibration the universe brings positive and interesting situations that you will make you smile and get excited.

3. ***Principle 3: You have the power to change your mood*** – if your day is not going so well, you have the power to change how you react to it. For example, your phone gets stolen in the mall, you can choose to be cranky and have a bad day, or you can choose to see a brighter day by believing that you will get a better one, and you will see that something good will come your way.

4. ***Principle 4: There are four steps to follow to create a deliberate action.*** 1. Identify what you don't want. Whatever you don't want, be wise enough to point it out. 2. Be

clear about what you want. 3. Create a feeling. Feel the way you would have felt if you have it 4. Avoid resisting or blocking. Allow the universe to do its job by bringing it your way.

5. *Principle 5: Allow the law of attraction to work* –once you have played your part, the law would take its turn, and if you have any doubt, results will be delayed. Keep feeling good, and the best will come your way just as the law of attraction predicts.

The more you love and desire something, great forces drive you towards achieving it both within and outside yourself. When you constantly remind yourself that you can actually achieve something, and you predict the outcome, then you have created the positive and repetitive power of proclamation of that thing which you desire to achieve. Because being able to create an image of a better future simply means you can actually bring that future into reality.

Logically, people always assume that people's attitude and judgment to things around them is a reflection of the information they get about the object in question and people's appraisal of things also reflects the information gotten about it. For example, the important factor in our judgment of people is the feeling they trigger in us. Knowing and emotions are linked together, which implies that our feelings or emotions are necessary to help us make decisions and keep our thoughts in order.

Positive thinking is a strong force in life. Life brings to us what we think about, and every time, we think and speak a word, it has to be positive because the world is listening, and it is responding. Learning how to use the law of attraction to improve your life is a process that takes time and needs patience to manifest. There are few ways in which you can put the law of attraction in use.

The first step is to take responsibility for the things that have occurred in your life, be it good or bad. This can be difficult to achieve as we are made to believe that our environment plays a major role in whatever circumstance we find ourselves in, but we should be able to help ourselves move past these events by writing down the events that had occurred in our lives previously, both good or bad. Go through them and discover that the events that occurred in your favor occurred at the time when positivity was all you thought about, and the things that happened against you were caused by negativity. When you have accepted responsibility for your fate, you can take a step further to determine what you wish to change in your life or what you want to achieve. Put them into writing, and keep checking them, constantly reminding yourself about them. Work towards them, and watch your dreams become a reality.

Another thing you need to understand is the law of vibration. Everything around you starting from the stars, planets in space, and even the sand on earth are all in a state of vibration, and you might not be able to understand this because everything around us is solid, but just because we are smart, our brain has been able to assimilate the vibrations around us and transform them into our reality. That is the reason why we can't recognize the earth's vibration. But come to think of it. If you studied science at some point in your life, then you should know that the colors we perceive and the sounds we hear are vibrations at a certain frequency that our brain has assimilated enough to make sense out of it. With this knowledge, your entire reality happens within your head, and this is the basis of the law of attraction. Let all your vibrations be positive, and be confident that your dreams will become a reality. This is a very important part of the law of attraction that you need to understand because your mind can wander easily into negativity, which may begin to send negative signals to your vibration. For you to create your reality positively, you have to believe that everything around you is vibrating. Keep every doubt out of your mind, relax, and feel the vibration in nature, in the sounds, and in the air around you.

You need to understand that like attracts like. The law of vibration states that similar vibration frequency is attracted to each other. For example, if two drops of water are moving towards each other, they get attracted to each other, get closer, and become one. However, oil and water can never mix together because they are of different minds. This reflects one of the logic behind the law of attraction.

Now that you know that everything around you is vibration, and they attract similar frequencies, the next thing you need to do is develop the ability to control your vibration and the things that happen in your life. It is better to always take out time to think about the ideas we create in our minds to know if they make sense. This way, we create our own reality. This explains the law of attraction that says positive thinking attracts positive thinking, while negativity attracts negativity.

Sometimes, people make mistakes when it comes to applying the law of attraction, but the good news is these mistakes can be corrected. Some of them are:

1. ***Believing positive thinking is enough.***
   Positive thinking alone cannot be enough
   to achieve your dreams and to put the law
   of attraction to use. Our mind operates on
   the conscious and subconscious level, so
   don't just think positively, you need to also
   put your thoughts in practice, and make
   them a reality.

2. ***Becoming impatient.*** You need to
   understand that for every action we take,
   there is an equal reaction to it. The world
   works according to its own speed, not
   yours, which means the science of the law
   of attraction may take time to reflect its
   fruitfulness. So, becoming impatient with
   the universe can create negativity within
   you which is bad for the law of attraction.
   Thus, avoid the mistake of being impatient.

3. ***Thinking you can determine how and
   when you will attract what you want is
   another mistake you should not make.*** It is
   not right to determine how or when you
   want to attract that which you desire since
   the universe has its own time of
   manifesting. If you take it upon yourself to
   choose when or how, it simply means you

have no faith in the law of attraction, so avoid this mistake by allowing the law of attraction to work for you at its own time.

When you avoid making these mistakes, the law of attraction will always work for you whether you believe in it or it. It's just like the law of gravity; you don't need to believe it to work.

CHAPTER 3

LOVE AND THE LAW OF ATTRACTION

"*Mind over body*"

This is a concept you must have come across at one point in life. And, in case, you are not familiar with it, here's a breakdown for you. The mind is not fixed. Some say it is in the heart (determination), and some say it is in the head (thoughts). Wherever it may be, it does play a huge role in decision making and reaffirmation of "gut feeling". Usually portrayed in movies as being strong enough to overcome physical pain, it is that Zen mode where all things flesh is made of becoming nonexistent, and the pain receptors which are linked to the brain are numb.

Now, how does the law of attraction tie up with

that saying? How can you be happy and even manifest love with this concept? All these and many more would be duly explained to you.

UNDERSTANDING THE CONCEPT OF LOVE

Scientifically, this is usually described as a release of a specific hormone called Oxytocin which sends a signal to the brain causing the person to feel extremely attracted to the same or opposite sex. You might beg to differ, so here's a universal description. Love is unexplainable. It is a strong emotional attachment to someone, and it could have been formed over varying periods of time.

Several cultures have different ways of expressing love. Some are expressive while others are not. This, however, does not stop the feeling of a sort of bond to exist between two or more people grow as it can foster trust. The earliest and truest form of emotional love is that which exists between a mother and her child. It is unexplainable and has been proven to be able to stand the test of time.

There are several forms of love. There is the agape love which is the love of the spiritual Father in the religion, Christianity. There is platonic love which usually exists between siblings and is known for the absence of lustful thoughts, and there is romantic love which exists between two people who are in a relationship and are intimately involved together, and so many more forms of love.

How to manifest love using the law of attraction?

A case study: A couple has been in a relationship for a span of three months, and every time, the man is usually open to spill his feelings and does not hold back on his emotions while the lady is a bit more controlled when it comes to professing her love. This, then, causes the more romantic partner to feel under-loved and could lead to a possible breakup depending on how they manage their conflict.

The law of attraction states that it is **Give and Take**. This means the amount of love shared is the same as one receives. For balance to be maintained, it has to be the same level on both sides. If you give out positive vibes, you will realize that your partner unconsciously does the same, and if you give off a negative vibe, then you should be ready to face the consequences.

Another case study of the power of thought in love is when one partner persistently gives reasons why they can't be perfect together. This causes them to notice the flaws of their partner and further cement their afore thoughts causing an eventual stalemate. Our thoughts have a big role to play in a lot of things that influence our choice including our relationships, and if not done right, they can result in the wrong decisions.

There are a few steps that can help you harness the power of law of attraction in your relationships.

1. *Focus on yourself first:* Thoughts are inborn, and before they are directed towards another medium, they must first come from within, and that is why the first step to manifest love using the law of attraction is to focus on yourself. Do away with any self-pity and negative thought that may come up.

2. *Focus on the positivity:* As the second case study has shown, a good vibe thrown in here and there can go a long way to a better relationship. Quit noticing the worst aspects of your partner, and tone down on the rollercoaster mind that is quite imaginative.

3. ***Be a cheerful giver:*** Though it is good to focus on yourself but do not deny someone the joy of realizing you love them just as much as they do. Be free with compliments, listen, and chip in as and when due. And when you do both, it puts you on the right path to quelling any self-centeredness that may arise.

4. ***Catch the Vibe:*** Well, if you are no stranger to soulmates, other halves, perfect match and a whole bunch of other catchy affiliations, then this shouldn't surprise you. When choosing the right partner to start something with, a vibe or common ground must be felt. This makes it easier to express love. When in a relationship with someone, be sure to be on the same frequency as that person.

5. ***Have a mental picture:*** The most practical thing to do is having a mental journey of what life would be like with the person. If you can clearly picture that without tons of "what-ifs" popping up in your head, then, you can be certain you are on the right path.

Why you have not been able to find love

In case you're trying to attract love, it's important to understand why it is that your efforts to find love have been fruitless. Everybody's love story is marginally unique. Notwithstanding, there are basic factors in play that can prevent you from finding the love you deserve.

For instance, you may relate to some of the points below:

•*You've shut down your mind unknowingly:* Subsequent to experiencing a heartbreak, a piece of you might attempt to shield your heart from future hurts. Unfortunately, this has stopped you from the possibility to discover love too.

•*You are still stuck:* It's difficult to attract love when you are still stuck on past relationships. Maybe, you have not completely handled an especially unpleasant relationship you had in the past. Or on the other hand, there's an old partner you think is difficult to forget.

•*You've lost hope:* When you've been searching for love for quite a while, you may quit trusting that your soulmate is out there. You might be tempted to make do with an "okay" relationship as opposed to focusing on a mission to discover love.

Notwithstanding, there are methods that can

show you how to show love when all is said and done or with a particular individual.

How to attract love.

In case you're hoping to figure out how to attract love quickly, the important thing you have to do is to begin to look for love with genuine expectation. This means you should figure out how to adjust yourself to a particular vibration that can draw in love as opposed to frustration, and that you have to build up a distinctive, clear feeling of what you're really trying to do when you plan to attract love.

Many of us never refine our idea of what searching for love implies. The universe can't enable us to discover love if we don't generally recognize what we really need. If you have ever thought of using the law of attraction in your love life, trust me, you are not the only one. The good news is using this law in finding a good and befitting partner works. There are proven physical advances you can take that has the power to boost your chances of attracting a partner really quick.

Here are a few tips:

Tip 1. Visualize Your Perfect partner

The same way it is possible to picture having more money, it is possible to picture a perfect partner. You do not have to get excessively explicit (like thinking of particular hair shade, style, most loved music band, and so on). Honestly, it is better not to give careful consideration to little subtleties like that, or you may end up making an insignificant rundown of qualities that looks increasingly like a shopping rundown and truthfully, nobody is perfect. Remember you are not attempting to pull in somebody who just looks great on paper only. You will need to consider pure love.

So, don't be excessively exacting, and center more around inquiries like: What might you find appealing about them? What will it feel like wanting to be with them? What might you do together? In trying to visualize your perfect partner, asking yourself the following questions can help you in making a definitive vision of the partner you want.

Get some information about your necessities and wants in your mission to discover love:

1. What 5-10 words would you use to portray what you truly need in a partner?
2. What identity qualities in someone else attracts adoration from you or help to draw out the absolute best in you?

3. How would you like to be treated by a partner? When searching for love, what are the practices that you will just never endure?
4. What are your most profound, most ardent interests throughout everyday life?
5. What do you consider to be your life's central goal?

Tip 2. Make a Dream Board about your love life

After creating a reasonable vision in your mind, you might need to make a physical note of what you are searching for, so it can feel a bit real to you. Making a dream board of whatever you want is very common in the application of the law of attraction. A dream board is basically a composition of suggestive pictures that help you to remember the thing you need to show. In light of this, create a board or space on your wall, and paste pictures (or different things) that constantly remind you that love is coming your way. You can cut pictures from magazines, use photos you've taken, discover things in the real world, make portraits, or simply set up expressions that truly catch your feeling of what love is about. Put this arrangement in a conspicuous spot, and ensure you take a look at it on different occasions daily. It should make you grin and feel confident whenever you start to lose hope.

Tip 3. Live Like You're loved

It will be simpler to show genuine, enduring love in your life the moment you can figure out how to begin to live as if you already have the love you are searching for. You may be somewhat hesitant while doing this kind of thing at first. Yet, it truly makes all the difference. Start small —for instance, you may purchase a card that says "Happy Anniversary Love" or a little, sentimental bit of gems that could be suitable for a birthday. Also, you can endeavor to keep up an attitude equivalent to knowing you're now in love. Smile more, tune in to marvelous music, and let every happy couple you see remind you of what you are hoping for in your life. Another important part of living the "as if" life includes changing your home to make it palatable for this new love you want to attract. You need your living space to depict your desires. In this way, think of where and how your partner may invest their energy in your home, and change things to all the more likely suit him or her. You may purchase another seat, alter your style, or get new bed-blankets that appear to be more fitting for a couple than a single person. While you trust that your love will arrive, you can likewise devote some portion of your home to doing your representations and different activities. You can do this in the extreme right corner of your room, and this part of your room is the place you ought to invest the vast majority of your energy when you're trying to practice the law of attraction.

Tip 4. Show Love Wherever You Go

Since the law of attraction instructs that "like attracts like", it shouldn't come as a surprise that pulling in love expects you to be a cherishing individual! Also, it's not just the sentimental feeling of love that is the issue here. There are easily-overlooked details that you can do to spread love each and every day—a standout among all is basically more pleasant to outsiders. For instance, you may offer cash to a beggar, offer help to an individual who is battling with an extensive box, or pay a genuine compliment to somebody wearing a lovely coat. These little activities show love and make the universe bound to give you love back. To send out more love vibes, consider volunteering a portion of your extra time to support a decent purpose. Be as imaginative as you like, and pick something that matters to you. You could go to a hospice and give the inhabitants a nice rose, gather pledges for philanthropy near your heart, or acquire a new skill, (for example, how to receive calls at an emergency telephone line). You'll definitely attract similar love, compassion, and cherishing thoughtfulness you're transmitting.

Tip 5. Avoid any Hindrance

Now that you are working on any mental and emotional blocks that can prevent you from attracting love, our main focus here is on physical advances you have to take. So, reflect on the things in your condition that may assume the job of physical hindrances to another person coming into your life. One of the clear hindrances that you might be ignorant of can be things that might suggest to a new partner that you are still stuck on your ex, it might be a cloth, objects you don't use, books that don't intrigue you, etc. If returning it to your ex might seem impossible to do, then think of some ways you can put them into use. For instance, you can give it out, or sell them online. Obviously, there are some cherished things from the past that can be very difficult to part with. For instance, think of important photos, old love letters, and unique remembrances from vacations. If at all, you would truly prefer not to discard these or let them go, you can reduce their impact on your efforts to attract love by putting them away in a crate that can't be seen and that won't clearly incite contemplations of earlier connections. Doing it this way causes you to focus on the future instead of the past.

Tip 6. Find an object that helps you connect to your expectations

Regardless of whether it's something you find at home or something that you go out and purchase, look for an object that in a flash makes you think of the perfect partner you know is coming into your life. Take this with you wherever you go, and use it as a reminder of the love you deserve. You can, likewise, hold it in your hands while visualizing, so it keeps you continually attached to your goals to have a new and loving relationship. Each time you see the object, let it help you to remember your trust, expectation, love, and satisfaction.

. . .

7 Extraordinary Ways You Can Attract A Particular Individual

Showing a connection with somebody is less demanding than you may think. When you move beyond any sentiments of sadness, despair, or any constraining convictions, the procedure is very straightforward and quick.

1. *Be certain about yourself:* Understand the extraordinary individual that you are and that it doesn't make a difference what others think about you. You don't need to make another person like you or adore you since you as of now cherish yourself. Self-assurance is compelling and will draw people to you.

2. *Concentrate on the positive:* Relinquish all your negative musings. For example, "For what reason don't they perceive how great I am?," and "Nobody will ever adore me." You have a ton of extraordinary characteristics that make you so deserving of anybody's adoration and consideration. Others do see you and welcome you. There is love surrounding you. Give it access. When you let it in and center around the

constructive, you change your vibration and open an entryway for the Law of attraction to present to you the person you want.

3. **_Love without dread of getting injured._** The scariest thing about affection is opening yourself totally. When you open yourself, there's a shot you may get injured. In case you're anxious about getting injured, you may unwittingly be keeping somebody from getting as near you as you need. Be eager to break yourself and completely open yourself to love. You will show the love you need.

4. **_Have a ton of fun._** Individuals are most pulled in to grins and giggles. When you're having a decent time, others notice and need to be with you. So do the things that fulfill you... regardless of whether it's viewing an interesting motion picture or heading off to your most loved park to have lunch. Make an amazing most of it. The better time and delight you have, the quicker you can pull in a particular individual.

5. ***See the positive.*** Concentrate on the beneficial things about the particular individual you want to attract. Search for something to appreciate. This can be extreme if there are negative sentiments among you, and you may just have the capacity to discover one thing first and foremost, yet in the event that you continue working at it, it will get simpler. In case you're involved with the individual as of now, you should begin to see his/her conduct change and things begin getting better between you.

6. ***Welcome the complexity.*** Be glad for what you have. Disregard the things that you are needing. When you can be upbeat at the time, the things you need will begin falling in place, including your love life.

7. ***Be happy to release the other individual.*** This is one of the hardest parts of the Law of Attraction for love while trying to attract a particular individual. You are very sure you want this person and now you are being told to be ready to let them go. Funny isn't it? However, it's only when you are okay with the thought of not being with

them that the law of attraction kicks in and start to work for you. Until you're alright with not being with him/her, a piece of you is opposing and making it outlandish for you to have what you need. This implies, as indicated by the Law of attraction, that until you're alright with potentially losing him/her, it will be hard for you to have the relationship you need with him/her.

Finding Love

A popular belief about the law of attraction is that it is charged towards interpersonal relationship and how to deal with people better. But that's not entirely true. It is also a tool for self-betterment, assertiveness, declarations, and reaffirmation of positivity that would lead to a manifestation of your desire which will consequently help in finding love. However, finding love is not as easy as it sounds. It takes dedication, focus, and acceptance.

Finding love means commitment and opening up yourself to positive thoughts. Consistency is also key as you continually open the flood gates to allow the energy to wash over you and thereby transfer them to your chosen partner. Focus on what you want, when and how you want it to be when you finally do. Focus on the good, a little on the bad, focus on being open and compromising as at when due. Focus on the present, stay happy for the moment, live for it, let it drive you and you're good to go. Accept the fact that it's possible to lose your partner along the way. It may hurt but the earlier you do the easier it is for you to move on if it actually happens. This way you use the law of attraction to help yourself, create a better version of you and find love

You probably won't discover love where and when you anticipated it. So you should keep a positive outlook and be aware of signs from the universe. These might come as fortuitous events, rehashed symbolism, or chance gatherings. Trust that your instinct can tell whether such potential signs are huge.

Living the "as if" life can be an incredible method to attract love. This means you should attempt to experience each day not just as you're searching for love but rather as if you've already discovered it! Show self-esteem, and dress as you would in the event that you were spending time with your partner. Endeavor to make space for them in your home. Consider your-self to be an individual with a cherishing perfect partner and a splendid future, and make arrangements appropriately.

In any case, whatever you choose to do, center around doing what fulfills you. Try not to stress over how things are with your partner constantly. Stress over yourself. Spoil yourself. Deal with yourself. The law of attraction will present to you the love you need.

CHAPTER 4

HAPPINESS AND THE LAW OF ATTRACTION

The utmost craving of every human is happiness. This is the reason we do the things we do, we take the jobs we take, we meet the people we meet, and we go to the places we go to. But it is common to see that some people are always not in a good mood like there is never a time or day you catch them smiling or laughing at anyone or anything. It always seems that these people have the whole weight of the world on their shoulders, with the way their shoulders are always slumped, eyes down-cast, face straight, mouth in a thin line, and jaw dropped.

This aura and countenance will make these kinds of people lonely and without friends. Either they are the one who push people off or people push them away, there is this constant fact that they hardly have people they are really close with.

And when you ask them what is wrong, you hear something like, "I am not happy". Pressing forward, you would find out that they most likely have issues with either their jobs, their careers, their finances, their families, their relationships, or their marriages.

Looking further, you find out that some of the things they complain to have issues with are things that some other people are battling with too, but you find out that there is a canny difference between these other people and the person you are dealing with.

This gets you pondering how and why these two categories of people, going through the same things in life, exhibit two different characteristics and attributes. While one is exhibiting traces of happiness, the other is always sad.

In answering this question, let's talk about what the concept of happiness is exactly, people's diverse definitions of happiness, and what defines happiness for different people.

WHAT IS HAPPINESS?

The definition of happiness is relative. Different people have different definitions of the concept. Let's take a look at a few of these definitions from people.

According to Sonja Lyubomirsky, Professor of Psychology at the California University, "Happiness is the experience of joy, contentment, or positive well-being, combined with a sense that one's life is good, meaningful, and worthwhile."

To Lara who lives in Germany, "Happiness means being content. It is living a moment fully, taking everything in, without comparing. It is a stage of doing, saying, or experiencing something wholeheartedly."

Natasha from Malaysia thinks, "Happiness is contentment in doing everything in moderation. It is in being delighted over an amazing sunset. It is in recognizing that life is too short for you to be either too upset or too excited when things go wrong or when it goes your way. Happiness is finding joy in giving. And it is in existing in such a way that you make it slightly easier for everyone you meet along the way. Kindness grows. It grows into happiness."

According to another unnamed source, happiness is when everything starts to fall in place. It could be something simple like making all the green lights on your way to school or when a relationship or job finally seems to work itself out for the best. It is when all you've always hoped for and worked for is right in front of you."

Based on the above definitions, it is quite obvious that although the effects of happiness are somewhat similar in everyone, and that contentment is the key to happiness, it is still obvious that causes of happiness in people differ.

For the unnamed person quoted above, the reason they feel happy is when everything they have hoped for falls into place, it might be in the academics, jobs, or relationship with other people.

But for Professor Sonja, Lara, and Natasha, it is a feeling of contentment in little things that really count like the sunset, in little victories, and in living in the moment.

If we follow these three women, they are the ones who really explain what happiness should be about. Happiness should be about contentment. It is being contented about life and everything about you.

The English Dictionary defines contentment as an experience of satisfaction and being at ease in one's situation, body, and/or mind.

This means that the state of being happy is triggered when one is at ease and satisfied with their lives, themselves, and the environment.

What Defines Happiness for Different People?

1. *Good Jobs*: Different folks are happy because of different reasons. For some people, they are happy as long as their jobs are going well, their pay is fine, and their bosses are not breathing down their necks.

2. *Perfect Relationship with God And Humans:* Some people's happiness is dependent on their relationships with God and their fellow humans. If they have a good religious standing and a splendid rapport with neighbors, friends, colleagues, and family members, then everything is okay, and they are happy.

3. *Robust bank account:* Happiness for some other people is when they are financially stable and buoyant, when they have the cash to buy whatever they need, anytime they want.

4. *Achievements:* Setting goals and dreams, and also meeting them is the source of some people's happiness. They are happy and all over the moon when they set targets and goals, and they achieve them.

5. *Doing the things they love:* For some folks, doing the activities they enjoy doing is what makes them happy, such as surfing

the web, playing games, visiting the
cinema, fishing, partying, golfing, reading,
or watching movies.

As long as some or all of these things are in place,
they are happy. But what happens when these things
are not in place? They get angry with themselves, their
environment, people around them, and life generally.
They become UNHAPPY and exhibit some characteristics such as:

1. ***They see Life As Being Hard On Them.***
   Unhappy people see themselves as victims
   of circumstances. They believe they are
   victims of circumstances, and they are the
   butt of life's jokes. They see nothing good,
   fulfilling, and interesting about their
   existence, jobs, families, and careers. They
   are always pessimistic about everything
   and are always looking for people to start
   pity parties with.
2. ***They Don't Trust Anyone.*** Unhappy
   people don't trust anyone. The fact is they
   don't even trust themselves. They believe
   someone is out there to cause damage and

hurt them. Hence, they shut people out, and crawl into their shells like snails.

3. ***They Focus More On Negativity Than Positivity.*** The unhappy man or woman is full of negativity. They don't see themselves making progress in life or anything they lay their hands to do. They always believe they are going to fail. Hence, they put in little or no efforts in whatever they are doing. When they finally make progress, they are still unhappy and unmotivated to do more. They focus more on their failures than their victories.

4. ***They Are Ungrateful.*** Instead of being grateful for the gift of life and the little things that they have, they complain of not having enough. They focus on their needs, forgetting to be happy for the things they have.

5. ***They Compare Their Lives To Those Of Others.*** Unhappy people compare their lives with the lives of their friends and colleagues, and they always find themselves lacking and lagging behind. This makes them resent people who they think are

doing better than them. They measure their achievements and victories with regard to others', and if they come short of others' success, they feel sorry for themselves.

6. ***They Are Scared Of Their Future.*** People who are unhappy tend to think of their future with dread and worry. They are scared to visualize their future. They think of the different things that could go wrong with their lives in the next second, minute, and hour.

7. ***They Can't Let Go Of Their Past.*** Even when they should have moved on from their past mistakes, unhappy people dwell in their pasts. They refuse to bury the past in the past and forge on. Unhappy people live their days in constant worry and stress, feeling hopeless, helpless, and tired of the kind of life they are living, not minding the effects of their unhappiness on themselves and people around them.

Side Effects Of Unhappiness

1. ***Unhappy People Don't Enjoy Life:*** Because their life is filled with too much negativity, worries, and doubts, unhappy people hardly enjoy life. They go around with a cloud over their heads.

2. ***They Don't Have Peace Of Mind:*** A mind clouded with too many problems and worries cannot be at peace. That is why unhappy people don't have peace of mind. Their mind is always on one issue or the other.

3. ***They Send Negative Vibes To Others:*** The saying goes that you can't give what you don't have. An unhappy person can never be a source of happiness and positivity to others. All they can ever exude are bad energy and vibes, causing people around them to be unhappy and miserable too.

4. ***People Stay Away From Them:*** No one wants to be associated with unhappy and miserable people. People would only be friends with people who are happy, joyful, optimistic, cheerful, and boisterous. And since there is a saying that you attract your kind, an unhappy person will only attract

someone like them, who won't do them any iota of good.

5. ***Good Opportunities Elude Them:*** As stated above, nothing good comes to an unhappy and dull person. No one wants to be business partners with an unhappy person. No one would want to introduce the new business in town to them. They miss opportunities for business deals, which can upgrade their lives and finances.

6. ***They Are Stagnant In Life:*** Stagnation is another effect of unhappiness. Unhappy people can't move forward in life because they are too busy battling with self-guilt, envy, self-pity, and a host of other depressing thoughts. So, while others are making progress, they are stuck in place, wishing things can be different when they are not even doing anything to make things different for themselves.

7. ***They Don't Have Good Health:*** Unhappiness is a disease of the mind. And when the mind is sick, it reflects on the body. Unhappiness causes immune systems and body parts to get tired, which can attract lots of diseases and illnesses

such as stroke, fatigue, arthritis, and even premature death.

Based on the aforementioned points, we can see that being unhappy is not a good thing. It pays to be happy than to be unhappy.

And all it takes to be happy is to appreciate the little things in life. To be happy entails appreciating the life you are living, appreciating the people around you, appreciating the fact that you are alive and breathing, appreciate little successes and achievements, and being open to exploring new things. To be happy, you don't need to have the whole world. You don't need to have all the money in the world in your bank account. You don't have to have everything working for you to be happy. Happiness is a state of mind. One thing that separates unhappy people from happy people is not the fact they don't have challenges in life or they have their lives working fine. If you think that is what differentiates them, then you are wrong. What separates them is their mindset, their beliefs, and their dedication to making the best out of whatever life throws at them. The happy person dwells on their mistakes, failures, and challenges, they learn from it, and move on to positive things. They don't dwell on thoughts that are not encouraging and inspiring. They don't wish their lives were better than what it is. They don't throw pity parties for themselves. They take their lives in their hands and rise above every challenge they come across in life. They don't feed their fears, they feed their faith. They are determined to do better and be better. They don't allow anything to weigh them down or change their focus. That is what separates them from an unhappy person. Also, happy people are CONTENT with how their lives are at present while vying to make it better. This is something unhappy folks don't know and understand. They fail to realize and understand that being happy goes beyond having everything; it is all about being content and finding happiness in the little things around us. True happiness exists when people are happy and satisfied with who and what they are and the things they do.

Like unhappiness, happiness has its own effects and advantages too.

Effects Of Happiness

1. *Everything Works For Happy People*: To the happy person, the universe is in the favor. Everything they do just works

because they have the right attitude to life. Even if things don't work the first time, it will surely work the second time.

2. *They Exude Happiness:* Because they are happy and joyful, the aura around them is that of joy and happiness. There is never a dull moment with them.

3. *They Attract Good Things And Good People:* Darkness attracts darkness, and light attracts light. Unhappiness attracts unhappy people, while happy people attract their kind. They attract optimistic people, people who are focused, people who know what they want in life and how to get it.

4. *They Attract Opportunities And Right Connects:* Because they are focused and they have the right approach to life, they attract the right business and career opportunities. The right people are drawn to be identified with them and to do business with them.

5. *They Have Good Relationship With God And Humans:* Happy people have a good rapport with their fellow humans and a

strong and blossoming relationship
with God.

6. ***They See Good In Everything:*** To the good,
   everything is good. To the bad, everything
   is bad. To the miserable, life is miserable.
   To the happy, life is beautiful and amazing.
7. ***Their Mind Is Fresh And Open To
   Countless Opportunities:*** A happy mind is
   one decluttered of worries, fears, doubts,
   and negativities, and this kind of mindset
   is the perfect soil for ideas and innovations.
8. ***They Are Successful:*** Following what
   Albert Schweitzer said, "Success is not the
   key to happiness. Happiness is the key to
   success. If you love what you are doing, you
   will be successful."

Happy people are successful people, because they
love what they do, and they put in their best to get the
perfect results.

HOW TO ALWAYS ATTRACT YOUR HAPPINESS.

If you are wondering how happy people remain happy
and unfazed in the midst of challenges and problems,
then the answer is this, "Happiness Is a Choice". This

is the main rule of the law of attraction. When they make a choice to be happy and focus on things that constantly make you happy, then you will definitely stay happy.

According to Steve Maraboli, "Sometimes life knocks you on your ass... get up, get up, get up!!! Happiness is not the absence of problems, it's the ability to deal with them."
1

Happy people deal with whatever they are served. They don't whine and bite their fingers feeling terrible. They take the bull by the horns and turn their stumbling blocks to stepping stones. The fact that happy people stay happy and undaunted doesn't mean life is serving them a different dish. They just CHOOSE to stay happy. This is why they are different, and they easily overcome these challenges. Anyone who wants to be happy needs to make that choice to be happy. They need to stop exuding the wrong vibes, because the universe responds to and reciprocate whatever vibes a person sends out (as per the law of attraction), and they need to create their own atmosphere for happiness.

Train your mind to see positivity in everything. Whatever happens, try to look at the positive side of everything that happens. No matter how bad a situation is, there is always a happy side to it. Focusing on the happy side of things will keep attracting happiness to you. Celebrate achievements and victories no matter how little they are. Even if it is small as you cooking a meal you have always been trying to, celebrate it. Always give yourself accolades, and praise yourself. Make a decision to be happy at all cost, no matter the challenges you face. Talk yourself up all the time. Don't give room for unwholesome thoughts. Tell yourself how awesome and amazing you are all the time. Don't allow boredom overshadow you. Integrate happy activities into your day. Do new things. Learn new skills. Take up new hobbies.

Have fun. Laugh. Do what makes you happy. Don't leave room for depression. Laughing is good medicine for the soul so try to do it as often as possible. Take it easy on yourself. Don't rush yourself to do things. Take your time, achieve things, and meet targets at your own speed and pace. Don't take the little things in life for granted. Appreciate the sunrise and sunset. Appreciate nature. Appreciate little moments that bring your laughter. Be grateful for everything. Avoid negativity. Don't dwell too much on your past mistakes and hurts. Forgive yourself and move on. Never allow anyone to rain on your parade. Don't allow anyone to make you feel bad about yourself. Be a giver. A giver is a receiver. Jim Rohn said, "Only by giving are you able to receive more than you already have. "

Also according to H. Jackson Brown Jr, "Remember that the happiest people are not those getting more, but those giving more." So, if you want to be happy, be more of a giver than a receiver. Always try to show yourself love. If you love yourself as a person, you won't find it difficult to love people around you. And another law of attraction is that when you send out undiluted and pure love to others, multiple folds of the love will be sent back to you.

Being happy is rewarding than being unhappy. No one attracts anything good, be it the right people or money by being unhappy and miserable. Happiness is a conscious choice. You choose to be happy consciously and deliberately despite the opposing factors of life. If you remain steadfast in your resolve not to break a sweat over anything you would see that everything will consciously work together for your sake. The universe will work its magic and create the right opportunities for you to excel at all you do.

CHAPTER 5

MONEY AND THE LAW OF ATTRACTION

The key to fulfillment and living a successful life lies in your understanding of a very powerful law known as the law of attraction. Simply put, the law of attraction postulates that we are capable of attracting or becoming whatever we are focusing on. Imagine the universe as an energy field of sorts where humans exist and function as magnets. Our emotions, dreams, and ambitions are items with magnetic properties and when we focus on any of these things, we become drawn to them, and eventually, they become our reality.

All thoughts become real eventually so if you maintain a negative focus, you would be stuck under a cloud of doom and gloom while a positive mentality would produce a positive reality. Leaving thoughts and emotions unchecked sends the wrong energy into the universe and attracts more unwanted emotions and events into your life.

So, how does one reap the benefits of this powerful law? Well, the law of attraction is in constant effect and can manifest across various facets of our lives. One of such areas is in the area of wealth and financial abundance. There are many obvious benefits of wealth in our lives. Money can ensure that we are happy and our living conditions are as comfortable as possible. When we have financial freedom, our dreams, goals, and ambitions become easier to attain because freedom lets us focus our mental energies on the things we truly want. Many individuals wish to enjoy the luxury of financial freedom because it frees them from the stress and burdens of paying bills, debts, and hard labor.

Unfortunately, there are many misconceptions around the idea of possessing money in abundance. Society would have you believe that being driven by a need to have extraordinary wealth is as a result of being greedy and selfish. People also tend to believe that the richest amongst us are simply exceptional in some way or that they obtained great wealth and finances through unscrupulous means or severe sacrifice. If you intend to be financially free, you have to restrict such negative mentalities. The law of attraction dictates that positivity breeds positivity, and this is a mentality that individuals who have achieved financial freedom have in common. They focus their minds on positive thoughts with respect to their goals, and then they take action.

You can learn how to build wealth and abundance by mastering a few exercises. There are several visualizations tools and techniques that can help you learn how to effectively harness positive money habits.

TIPS FOR ATTRACTING MONEY AND WEALTH

"Remember always, money is a servant; you are the master."- Bob Proctor

Using the right techniques, it is possible to manifest wealth within a short period. Some experts say that 7 days is enough to manifest anything. The process might not have the same level of simplicity for some, but constantly working and fine-tuning your thoughts would eventually reap positive results. Don't give up. Financial success is a common gateway to other forms of success, and even if abundance is not your main goal, you will surely benefit from attracting some money into your life regardless.

Tip 1: Focus on Abundance

The law of attraction is totally based on the premise that you attract more of what you focus on. Simply put, financial abundance would not take effect in your life if you do not have a burning desire to achieve it.

Build your focus by setting a clear intention, and be specific about how much you want. Sincerely desire to have abundance, and be prepared to settle for nothing less. Eliminate the poverty mindset and begin to act as if you have money. Learn about new and interesting ways to invest and make money. Additionally, be grateful for what you already have. The more time spent focusing on the abundance you already have could lead to more coming your way.

Practice these tips by:

1. Creating a money board where you paste pictures of the things you intend to do or purchase with money. It could be a new apartment or a new car, some fresh clothes for the kids, or a much-needed vacation.

Find pictures of these things, and paste them on your board. Look at the board often, and remind yourself that you already possess these things.

2. Keeping a logbook where you note down the things you are grateful for on a daily basis.

Tip 2: Reverse Engineer your Thoughts

Negative thoughts will constantly arise when you are trying to attract abundance. It is common to tell yourself you can't do it. Sometimes, you might even wonder whether you deserve to be wealthy. However, your mind should be working in your favor and not against it. You can counteract this mentality by developing a mindset of manifestations that reverse your thoughts.

For example, when the thought that you will never be smart enough to make money crosses your mind, firmly begin to establish affirmations that begin with the ''I''. Tell yourself things like, "I can be successful," and "I can make huge amounts of money". Doing this will fixate your mind on the present, and it will begin to match your current reality with the reality that you affirm or wish for.

You can also use thought-stopping techniques like consciously saying the word "STOP" when you start to experience distorted or negative thoughts.

Tip 3: Spend Wisely

Figuring out the best ways to spend the money you already have is another great way to attract money. Much pleasure can be derived from spending money in a manner that aligns with your values. Doing this also helps to develop a positive relationship between you and money. When you have only positive thoughts about money, you will attract more of it instantly.

Besides, how will you manage huge sums of money if you have difficulty managing the little amounts you have now? Learning to manage and spend wisely will make it easier for you to boost your wealth in the future as you will see money as a servant rather than a master.

Tip 4: Get Real with Yourself

Money can bring total freedom and happiness, but

that is not all that manifesting wealth is about. Take the time to look at the reality of your finances and assess the situation with all honesty. Are you in debt? How high are your expenses? Do you need to revise your spending habits? Ask yourself the hard questions, and don't be afraid to ask for help if you need it. Family and friends can come in handy when the situation is dire.

Additionally, don't compare yourself to others. We all have different trajectories in life. Your current station is exactly where you need to be. Remind yourself that you can only get to where you want to be if you accept and acknowledge the truth about where you currently are.

Tip 5: Eliminate the Fear of Success

It is common to be afraid of failing, but it is equally possible to fear success. You could be afraid of what might happen or what things will change or how your success might affect your relationships. Fear is a hindrance to positive thinking and eventual abundance. Get rid of the fear of success by:

1. Questioning your fear: Ask yourself what success means to you. This will help you get a better grasp of what it is you are

afraid of. Define your vision for personal and professional success. Figure out how you will know when you are finally successful. What will you do? How will you behave?

2. Think about why you may be afraid of success: Try to understand the reason for your fear. Could it be because of past errors? Is it as a result of your social settings? Write down your reasons, and for each one, try to figure out where it came from.

3. Determine the extent to which fear is affecting you: Be honest with yourself about just how far you would have been if you weren't afraid. Write down examples of moments when you let fear sabotage your efforts.

4. Consciously declare defeat over fear: Write a statement declaring that you will never let fear destabilize you or stop you from reaching your goals anymore. Read your statement out loud. Doing this will help to boost your confidence, and it will serve as a reminder that fear has no power over you.

Tip 6: Meditate

Meditation has proven benefits ranging from stress management and relaxation to lower blood pressure and improved mental health. It is also an effective way to manifest wealth and abundance. Meditation harmonizes your mind with the reality of your abundance by creating a positive image about wealth and giving you a clearer picture of what your goal should look like.

The following steps outline how to use meditation to attract wealth and abundance:

1. Find a comfortable and quiet place, and sit down cross-legged or in a chair with your feet on the ground. Do this just before you go to bed.
2. Take deep breaths. Inhale and exhale while counting to ten each time. Do this five times. Imagine the tension and stress of the whole day leaving your body through your head, chest, waist, legs, and feet.
3. When you feel fully relaxed, imagine a warm, golden light filling you up.

4. Let a few minutes pass, and then begin to imagine money raining down on you. Imagine having so much of it that you no longer have space in your room. Imagine sharing with friends and family.

5. Allow joy and fulfillment to possess you. After a few minutes of basking in the euphoria, slowly open your eyes.

6. Perform this meditation steps regularly before you sleep, and once you get the hang of it, you can start to repeat it more times daily.

8 SIGNS THAT INDICATE YOU ARE ABOUT TO MAKE SOME MONEY

If you have been working towards a financially abundant life, you might be curious to know when your efforts will be rewarded. Throughout history, there have been certain signs that indicate the universe is about to send you money. These signs are equally handy when you want to make an investment or begin a new venture.

1. You constantly come across the number 8

2. You get money on symbolic days or holidays
3. Bugs keep showing up around your house
4. When you are expecting a baby
5. You have lots of loose change
6. Bubbles in coffee
7. You see your initials in a spider web
8. An unpleasant run-in with a bird

CHAPTER 6

YOUR HEALTH AND THE LAW OF ATTRACTION

Health concerns pervade every facet of our existence. These health challenges are not peculiar to a group of people. Like the law of attraction, health concerns occur regardless of nationality, age, and even religious beliefs. The laws that guide and govern the universe influences everyone. It leaves an impressionable impact. Whether you believe in it or not, we attract what we focus on. No matter the health concern, whatever you imagine or focus on with your mind's eye can have a healing effect. Be positive to push your body and condition to a better standard.

The law of attraction is such a great and powerful force that if used properly, it could be life-changing.

This law has long been in existence, and only those who understand its secrets can benefit. It goes beyond the physical and often times the rational. That's because you have to believe in it to have that transformation. It's upon us to attract into our lives the thing or feeling we focus on. This may take different shapes. Some simply want the law of attraction for money, health, love, and so many other things. A firm grasp of this natural phenomenon will set you on the path you crave.

Negative thoughts harm and poison the body. The fact is the positive mind heals the body faster than any drug or therapy known to medicine. Consistent negative thoughts will breakdown your body systems faster than a terminal disease. It's like handing out a death sentence to yourself. The manifestation of the disease deprives you of the much-needed strength to fight back.

You can experience the best of health by being downright positive. You have to think and act as though your desires already exist. By this, you're actively taking control of your thoughts and life. The energy we give off attracts similar energy. That means negative energy will attract a negative outcome. If you can envision and act on positive health, you will have it.

Sometimes people ask, "Can health issues be reversed through positive thinking?" The short answer is "yes". There's no condition too difficult for the law of attraction to alter. The fact is it's all in mind. Our attitude, attention, and response to the power of the universe over our sickness is important. You could be going through any type of illness. Whether it's as minute as a common headache or as debilitating as cancer, whether it's depression or anxiety, be rest assured that it can be reversed or addressed. All you need to do is let go of the negative thoughts of such sicknesses. The negative feelings and thoughts must be replaced with good thoughts.

Good and positive thoughts work wonders for the body. For instance, if you have a cold sore and can't seem to get rid of it, you can focus on wellness. The results can be quite stunning because the universe puts your desire into play. When you think about the sickness all the time, you're unwittingly manifesting it. It cloaks your ability to manifest good things and through that the sickness fosters.

HOW TO GET BETTER HEALTH USING THE LAW OF ATTRACTION?

There are a number of factors that add up to grant you your earnest desires. Observing them will go a long way in healing that deformed mind and infirmed body. Here are some of the most important factors to consider:

Figure Out What You Want For Your Health.

If you don't know what you want, you're going to attract what you don't want. It's that simple. Focus on getting better. Do you want to be stronger or for the illness to go away? Perhaps, you just wish to be stronger to fight on. In essence, the point is you have to be specific with those thoughts. It's not a random act of luck or favor. Having a clear plan and ways to achieve the desired outcome also helps. Realizing where you've gone wrong and thoughts that have held you back from a full recovery is equally important. It's vital so that you find ways to steer off the negativity. It's okay to walk into the unknown. To try something new and unique. Conventional medicine can only go some way. Genuine health and the joy that comes with it is available to you. Do your best to access it by knowing what you want.

Have The Conviction You Will Be Fine.

We can seldom get things done without believing them deep within us. It's that inner conviction that helps us manifest what we want. You have to believe or have faith that your body is well and healed. When you want something and proceed to ask for it, you have to know it has been given or released. You only need faith to access it and enjoy the health benefits that result. Sometimes, the infirmity leaves us with serious doubts and concerns about our well-being or health. We can't have two or varying opinions in our minds and hope to experience better results. Believe is just as important as knowing what you want. Have a conviction that the universe is conspiring to favor you. For instance, if you're about to undertake a medical procedure, believe that you're coming out of that situation unscathed and healthy. Even if it's a broken limb, you attract quicker healing by believing. Law of attraction is an effective tool when accompanied by faith.

Affirmations Are Key.

Ever heard people say words like "I'm healed," "I feel no pain," "I'm healthy and fine"? These are words of affirmation spoken out of a belief that things will favor them. They sound weird, but the fact is it will make them better and healthy. Also, these type of words repeal the negative statements and thoughts we have. Focus on what you want for your health and write it down. This helps you remember and say aloud the words that can transform your health. Some people also answer in the negative when asked about their health. They offer statements such as "I can't bear the terrible pain," or "It's so bad. I think it's getting worse." Those are deadly words straight from the inside. How do you expect to heal or get better when your confessions are negative? The universe hears us, and the mind and spirit are left sunken from such irrationality. We may feel we are honest, but the fact is words like those mean we embrace the condition. Do well to be positive with your thoughts, actions, and affirmations.

Visualize That Perfect Health.

If you have strong imaginations, use them positively. Picture yourself in optimum health conditions. Go beyond the limits. Envision yourself doing all the things the physicians said couldn't be done. Visualize yourself walking, talking, running, or jumping. Remember the law of attraction has no boundaries. All your positive actions will draw and release positive energy into your body. As a result, your health begins to benefit. If your imagination can't do enough, other techniques of visualizing exist. They include drawing and painting. If it's something your mind's eye can see and it's positive, let it grow. Visualize all the possibilities associated with a healthy person who doesn't have your condition. You only have to feel positive about what you're trying to manifest. Don't let the strange looks and stares deter you from acting out your desires. Visualizing is a strong weapon of the law of attraction. Don't be vague about what health means to you. Be clear with your dreams, visions, and imagination. That good health you wish to have will not be elusive for long. Forget about doubts. You've already received what you imagine from the universe.

Don't Let Worry and Stress Overwhelm You.

Sometimes our health concerns and sickness get us all worked up and stressed. While it's okay to feel that way, we must not let it go unabated. If you're worried about your health, you can replace such thoughts with positive ones. Worry impedes the goodness of the universe from coming your way. The law of attraction is powerful and effective. That stress and constant worry will only make things worse. Personal questions you should ask yourself include: "Will worrying improve my condition"? "Has worrying helped me out before"? "What am I attracting by worry"? You'd certainly be attracting bad omens and more bad health. Worrying will increase your stress levels. If you already had an ailment, you'd be adding high blood pressure to the list. This will break you down faster than any illness. Try to de-stress by getting rid of situations that make you worry. Some patients heal faster when they genuinely let go of worry and embrace the joy's the universe releases. Choose to be a bundle of faith and happiness. Willfully smile, and let the law of attraction take its full course. Again, you shouldn't dwell on your injury, sickness, and medical conditions. Meditation has been proven to help relax your mind and body. Meditation won't take all your time. A few minutes are fine provided you actively participate and ease out the tension.

Mingle and Associate with Healthy People.

That's what you want to be right? Healthy. It can

only help if you stay around healthy people more. In fact, you're being commanding of your situation. When you are sick, and you move around all day with other sick people, you're likely to remain that way. You get to feed off that negative energy they transmit. Again, seeing close friends and family makes you want to be strong for them. It boosts your psyche when you have these happy moments. When you spend more time with healthy people, you automatically attract better health. You find yourself thinking along the lines of being like them. Being able to walk and speak freely. These are positive thoughts of wellness and health. It also means less time on your hands to worry about yourself and your health. Expect excellent responses from the law of attraction when such inter-actions give you better feelings. It doesn't just stop at associating with people. You also have to be mindful of what you read and watch. For instance, someone who suffers a fracture shouldn't watch a medical show with extreme scenes. They won't add value or help you get better. You have to be careful not to send the wrong message out to the universe. Positive energy is worth its weight in gold. Conversely, good programs that encourage healthy living can be watched or listened to.

· · ·

Show Genuine Gratitude for Things, Yourself, and People.

The law of attraction responds well to thankful minds and spirits. Being thankful for what you have is not an uphill task. It is a good start and shows that you appreciate the favor the universe has released upon your life and by extension, your health. You'll feel a whole lot better when you offer thanks to people for the love and kindness they've displayed towards you. Whether that's with words or gestures, it strengthens your mindset. It's a positive way to go about your life. It also helps you worry less. Again, you'd be amazed at the number of things you can be thankful for when you write them down. It's okay to be thankful for your healthy body. It's an affirmation that will stick in the long run. It's better than being sad every day for a sickness you can do very little about. You can do something about that attitude though. Change it. You can look on the mirror and say repeatedly, "I'm genuinely grateful for my perfect health and body." You can also set apart each day for something new to be thankful for. This will increase positive vibrations and this, in turn, attracts good health.

The key to harnessing the power of the law of attraction for your health is to always make a conscious decision to have joy and happiness. It may be hard at first, but you have a lot to gain. Move on from people too focused on your health for all the wrong reasons. Let positivity be your watchword and mantra. Your health will sync well with the law of attraction when you have a happy and positive demeanor.

CHAPTER 7
POWER OF POSITIVE THINKING

I t is no news that your well-being is 100% determined by you. Your life is a ship, and no one else but you are the sailor of that very ship. Therefore, allowing any and every one sail that ship is a matter of **CHOICE** on your path. This could either be as a result of carelessness on your part or laziness. But all of these can change if and only if you give way to the transforming power that can be generated from your mind through your thoughts to your body.

All these do not negate the existence of struggles, unforeseen and uncontrollable events, obstacles and tragedies, but in all of these, there is a force that can dominate all despite their existence and occurrence. When you give room for change in your day to day activities, through the positive power generated from your mind through your thoughts, you will easily rise above all these negative forces you never thought had breaking points. You also must know that although obstacles, hardships, and tragedies have the ability to break you, they were not designed to break you but rather mold you into a formidable force and personality of high positive resistance.

Giving into the positivity that emerges from the power that your thoughts does so many things to you like increasing your self-esteem, creating the necessity for self-improvement, highlighting your self-worth, making you likable, increasing your span of influence, making you useful, and keeping you healthy (both physically and mentally).

You are about to embark on a journey to a new, fresh, improved, and developed life which would result in a powerful you. We are going to talk about how having positive thoughts can bring out all of these changes in you.

Self Confidence

Your success and happiness in life lie in the confidence you have in and about yourself. How do you see yourself? What's the image you portray to people about you? How do you carry yourself around people? All of these questions are self-confidence tests that you must carry out. If you don't see yourself as good, others will have no choice but to view you via the same lens. (There might be exceptions, but you might never recognize those exceptions if you don't have the right image about yourself). You alone have the power and right to create the right and perfect image of **YOU.** You must learn to believe in the worth and value of every and anything that projects out of you. When you fail to have such level of confidence in yourself, you experience a sense of insecurity which becomes an obstacle to achieving the goals you have set for yourself in life and the achievements you have planned to attain. When you follow the right and healthy steps of attaining self-confidence, you exempt yourself from the hurdles and ditches created and dug by life as well as its miserable experiences. For you to know yourself, you have to create the perfect image of **YOU,** and for you to do this, you need to know why you feel inferior and also know yourself.

Inferiority Check

Carrying out this particular check, you must be completely ready to devote your time, and you must be ready to tell yourself the truth especially in areas you've lied to yourself about yourself. Feeling inferior is a stage every human on earth has experienced or passed through at one point of their lives or the other. Some get through that stage building strong and healthy self-esteem while others get overwhelmed and overpowered by those same experiences and stay dejected and contented with their lives. But hey! It isn't the end of the world for you. It's in fact, the breaking of a new dawn. If you still fight inferiority complex, remember you are on a journey to find some of the reasons for inferiority complex and proffer a solution or solutions to build healthy self-esteem. The below factors can be responsible for inferiority complex in life:

1. **Societal Approval:** This factor can be reflected through gender inequality, racism, religious ideologies, family background, economic status, etc. Society generally has ways of creating an unhealthy sense of making people want to belong. This validation from the society

pressurizes its citizens in an unhealthy way to want to live fake lives, which could lead to depression and dejection

2. ***Mental Discrimination***: This happens when unfavorable and unhealthy comparisons are being made regarding the successful achievements of a person in reference to another's average or poor performance. Such unfavorable comparison can affect the mental capability of a person, watering down your initial energy to want to work more.

3. ***Physical Disabilities***: At times your skin color, height, facial defect (eye, dentition), or body weight has its way of making you ashamed of your image in the public.

4. ***Childhood Experiences***: Rigid parenting, negative reactions, and remarks from your parents due to some childish actions you displayed have a way of dampening your self-confidence.

After knowing the basic causes of your inferiority complex, you can now go on to find how to get your confidence back. Trying out the following helps you build your self-confidence:

1. ***Know Yourself***: Genuinely love yourself, especially if you have physical disabilities. Stop comparing yourself to or with any and everyone. You are INTELLIGENT, SMART, CREATIVE, and UNIQUE. YOU MUST NOT FORGET THESE WORDS.

2. ***Know Your Strength***: Start to find out your strong points, your specialties, what you can do, and love to do. Begin to recognize those features that give you value and make you stand out in the crowd.

3. ***Create Healthy Relationships***: Get yourself away from people around your life who drain your happiness, who never appreciate anything and everything about you. Stir up meaningful relationships with people who celebrate your every effort. This might be hard, but it is a NECESSITY.

Know Yourself

This, in itself, can be hard especially in cases where you must have never seen anything good or encouraging about yourself due to the opinions people have given you. For instance, when you do make-up, you should make use of your hand and not someone else's. In the process of applying make–up, you begin to spot the beauty of your face. How your face is shaped, your pointed nose, small black eyes, sweet dimples, and your small lips. Celebrate yourself wherever and whenever no one does. Rebuke yourself where you've overlooked before and also appreciate yourself when you put efforts into making a better YOU. When you know who you are, you live a happy life, and when you can express your desire, you would be able to achieve a lot of set goals. Knowing who you are gives you a positive drive towards making meaningful decisions and making choices that are of great benefits to you and giving you guidelines on how to solve issues you have. Also, when you know yourself, you literally will have control over yourself, resisting negative habits, developing good ones, and also strengthening your values to the point where you can manage both internal and external pressure, which has a way of affecting your relationships with people.

Always Be At Peace

When your mind is at peace, you stay healthy. You can have peace of mind when you make your mind expel all of the negative thoughts, unhealthy emotional junk that has built certain parts of your life in the wrong direction. When you do this, there tends to be a release of freshness from your inside, and you, literally, will begin to feel light. This particular feeling usually is experienced especially when you let out your fears, hurts, guilt, insecurity, and regrets to some you truly trust. Emptying your mind of all those negative thoughts and energy is one step to being peaceful. The human mind can never stay empty for a long period of time. It is one of the busiest parts of the human system, so it will always want to get things to store. This is why you make no delay after emptying it of all the emotional junks. You can begin to fill it with positive images of yourself and even people around you, and one way, this can happen is by having a list of positive things you would want to see manifesting in-house life, you can place them on your wall, read them out loud, and watch your life take a new turn over a period of time. When you do this, those things you have flushed out of your mind would want to find their way back into your mind, but when they do, your mind would be too occupied with creative, healthy, and positive thoughts that would render you past mind occupants homeless. You obviously like the sound of that, but the homelessness can only be permanent when you constantly keep your mind occupied by thinking health and positive thoughts. In the course of this project of peacefulness, a serenity environment would be an amazing idea, a place where you could positively speak out to yourself those words of healing, positivity, and peace.

Finding inner peace also includes you staying away from places and people who only emit negative thoughts, words, and ideas. Such atmospheres have ways of triggering the return of those tenants you evicted (insecurity, hurt, fear, hate, and anger). Words have an intentional effect on your thoughts especially the words that come from you.

Customize Your Happiness

Being happy is a CHOICE – you choose to either be happy or unhappy. No one can make you happier than you would ever make yourself. Happiness is the easiest of all accomplishments in the world, and for you to be happy, you must put your mind into it. You must consciously fill your mind with happy thoughts. Go about confessing those thoughts audibly to yourself. Even when things are not going the way they ought to, never settle for them, tell yourself things can only get better. You are the force behind your happiness. Also, you can be the force behind your unhappiness – even in sad moments, develop happy thoughts by saturating your mind with happy thoughts. You can create happy thoughts by picturing your achievements being attained, your goals being achieved, and your needs being met. You customize your happiness by showing love first to yourself.

Expect Nothing But The Best

Never put up the thoughts of you not qualifying for anything good or perfect in your mind. You are deserving of every and anything that is perfect. Believing in yourself is what makes and configure your mind to succeeding. Believing is an important factor and a necessary force for success. Belief is an attractive force that pulls anything and anyone that is tagged best to your life. When your mind is saturated with self-belief, you will begin to expel positive forces that replace anything negative that might want to contend with your mind. Self-belief is the most powerful force in the world, and it's a free gift that has been given to you by God. Things turn a new leaf for the better when you think and believe that only the best can come and will come to you. A man of positivity is hard to distract.

. . .

Never Accept Defeat

When you think defeat, you already are defeated. You have to develop the attitude of never accepting defeat. Consciously get rid of any thought that has made you picture yourself as defeated. Your subconscious can be much of a deceiver at times, especially when it's introduced to a new system of development. Whatever you over-emphasize in your mind becomes an accepted conviction in your mind. This is simply explained that whatever becomes a conviction in your mind becomes your physical image. At times, negative thought patterns mixed with inferiority complex have a way of stimulating a defeat conscious life, so you have to be mentally equipped and prepared with right tools to knock out negative forces and negative convictions with positive thoughts and convictions. You can do this by emphasizing and over emphasizing a life of victory – a life void of defeat. When you allow new thoughts to flow through you, you will experience newness and freshness. Never forget that your thoughts make you, your mind is the powerhouse of your life, and positive thoughts guarantee a healthy and happy life.

REASONS WHY YOU NEED TO THINK POSITIVELY

To Awaken Your Happiness: Happiness here doesn't entail in your material possessions, but it is rather a state of mind or an attitude you have come to adopt by being positive. This has nothing to do with the happenings around you but the events that take place within you.

To Attain Success: Positive thinking guarantees you a successful life, and it serves as a propelling force to drive you towards achieving your dreams and set goals. It serves as a motivation to get things done in an excellent and easier way. This actually helps you overcome life's obstacles. It also strengthens your belief in yourself and in achieving what you thought could never be achieved.

Boosts Your Self Worth: When you adopt a life of positivity, it changes how you think and feel about yourself, giving you a better opinion of your image, thereby creating a high level of self-esteem. Seeing what is unique about you and celebrating it gives people a healthier and better view on you – causing them to treat you with a high sense of regard and value. Self-worth or self-esteem comes on the strength of loving yourself – this stirs up self-confidence, courage, and boldness.

Creates Healthy Relationship: Healthy thinking has so much of an effect on how you relate with people. People naturally are drawn towards you when you are a positive thinker. This is because a positive thinker is like a magnet. Be deliberate, intentional, and dedicated to saturating your mind with happy thoughts and positive thoughts alone, because the power you generate from your mind strengthens you. You must try to be as positive as possible for your mind to be able to cope more and better with stress. On your path to a life of positivity, you will encounter disappointments you have to deal with, which are likely to get to you in no small way. Positivity helps you manage such ugly and unfavorable moments. Positive thinking brings you out of the mood of wanting to accept and live a life of dejection, frustration, and anger. It gives you a drive that things never stay still for long. There is always a moment when they get to change. Positivity creates ideas on how you can change the situation of things for the better.

Your health is dependent on the strength and power of positive thoughts. Your well-being is impacted gravely by how healthy and how positively you think. It helps the health of your heart. With a life filled and saturated with positive thoughts, you become bold in facing hard situations, crisis, and even concussion. It gives you the initiative of always wanting to fix things when they go bad in order to restore hope and life to whoever is being affected. Positive thinking isn't being too proud or going to get yourself entangled in a situation bigger and beyond your capability. Rather, it is you seeing the good that can come out in every event even disappointments and also improving the situation and learning from them.

With all that you've read so far on this journey of positivity, you will agree that your life's quality and longevity is dependent on the thoughts that rule your mental world. Your mind needs to be sound for your body to be sound. Whenever you see positivity, think of soundness, health, life, newness, freshness, bold-ness, courage, and so many more. You and you alone have the power to change your life by reorienting your mind on what it should think of and what it should flush out. Your mind can work on its own without guidelines, so whatever becomes a frequent image in your mind gradually becomes a permanent conviction which would take a whole lot of unlearning to flush out.

Whatever it is you feel can help you generate positive thoughts which will flow all over your body. If you get the positive drive from reading, do it. Open the door of your mind, and expand its borders by pumping in relevant, sensible, and life-changing thoughts into it. If taking a walk helps you, do not hesitate. Take that walk today, and talk to yourself as you do so. Remind yourself about all of your uniqueness and specialties, about how creative you are, and how well the world needs you. Being alone actually helps positive thinking. If you see this as your best way of developing and channeling your best of thoughts and ideas into your mind, create such atmospheres for yourself. You could choose to add the mirror as a tool to look at yourself in the face and talk to yourself.

You are the one with the best of words that can either make or break you, add value and worth to your life today, and the world will come running to you. Never see yourself as small, incapable, or useless. The world needs you, and that's why you exist in it. So, get up from that position of negativity, look yourself in the mirror, and say to yourself:

I am beautiful. I am handsome. I am strong. I am unique. I am courageous. I am amazing. I am creative. I am a solution. I am a hope giver. Repeat all these sentences frequently.

CHAPTER 8
WORDS ARE POWERFUL, SPEAK IT

Words, as easy as they come out, remain one of the most powerful weapons in the universe. They seem too insignificant to make a change, and most times, the importance attributed to the usage is seen as rather unnecessary. But they are almost as important as life itself because they have a certain control over life that cannot be overlooked, no matter how hard we try. Words have set in motion many a time a chain of reactions that the speaker did not think possible at the time the words were spoken.

A good illustration of the existing power of words would be Christianity and its belief in the creation story. If you go through the story, you would see that words were greatly used. "Let there be light, let there be animals" a whole of lot things were brought to life by words. John 1:1 clearly states, "In the beginning was the word and the word was with God and the word was God." Words set in motion the world as they know it. So as much as we want to believe that words do not matter as much as they are said to, we are tugged daily by the truth, which is that they matter greatly.

As far as the law of attraction goes, we bring things that happen to us in our lives by our thoughts and our words, but most importantly by our words. You speak what's in your mind. But how about if you spoke differently, if what was in your mind was weighing you down, and instead of dwelling on these bad thoughts, you spoke something positive, something with better energy?

During a leader's conference once, the speaker, while trying to instill the power of positive speaking practically in the minds of the listeners, asked them to do a small game with numbers.

"Just count one to ten in your mind. While counting in your mind, if I ask a question, answer me, and get back to counting. Am I clear?"

The crowd answered in the affirmative.

"Now get on with it," he said. They began to count. After a few seconds, he asked, "who is the president of America?" They all stopped, and in unison, they answered "Donald Trump." He looked at them for a while and asked, "What number did you stop at?" They did not remember.

Screaming 'Donald Trump', had somehow truncated their thoughts on the numbers they already had in their mind.

He clapped excitedly and went on...

"You see, when you wake up thinking bad thoughts, and you are worried about how the day will go, about how impossible it would be for you to go through the day because of how you're feeling, you immediately speak up and say; I will get through this, today will be a good day! I am not limited by anything I feel. And there you go, it will be a pretty awesome day! You will be just fine. You know why? Because you have truncated that bad thought with good words."

Words can bring to life emotions that you thought were dead. They have the power to kill and make alive. They have the power to motivate, to get you out of a bad mood, and to put you in one also. They have the power to deal with issues you felt you could not deal with, telling yourself you can handle it subconsciously moves you in the direction of the much-needed solution.

Words are an underappreciated currency, the

value of which we most times ignore. The words you say to yourself have a lot of impact on your self-esteem and confidence. If we place as much value on words as we are supposed to, it would sincerely help us to be better. Our thoughts are important, but our words make up for the better part of what we attract into our lives.

THE POWER OF NEGATIVE WORDS

On a rainy evening, a girl was walking on a narrow bridge between muddy water and an overflowing gutter. She had walked on this bridge a few hours earlier. It had not rained then, but she walked on the bridge anyway just for the fun of it. This time when she was coming back, she had to use the bridge because it was flooded all around her. While she was using this bridge the second time, she said, "I'm in the danger of falling either inside this gutter or inside this muddy water." No sooner had she finished saying these words, she fell right inside the gutter. She got out of the gutter unhurt but had dirt all over. As she grew, she realized that she caused what had happened to her that day. She had passed that bridge success-fully before and was doing it again until she spoke negative remarks and the universe reacted in accordance with what she had spoken to it. She called, and the universe answered.

What she said was not exactly a very serious statement. As a matter of fact, it could be looked at as something insignificant, but it attracted an equally insignificant negative reaction to it. For every time you moan, complain, or whine about the situation of things around you and about the things that should be that are not, you are subconsciously setting off negative vibes. You are calling the universe with a voice of negativity, and it will answer, either quietly or loudly, but it will answer, and you will feel the answer manifesting in your life. You will suddenly begin to attract in large or small numbers the things you whine about. When you speak, you are sending a vibration around you, and this is setting things in motion, so when you speak negatively, you are sending this negative vibration around you, and it would not go setting in motion positive things. It will set in motion negative things because that's what it's attracted to.

Every time you wake up saying, "I don't feel good about today. I woke up on the wrong side of the bed," your day will react to what you said first thing in the morning, and by night, you would have had an unproductive day, where everything that could go ever wrong went wrong in about 16 hours. And all these happenings were reacting to these words, "I don't feel good about today."

These negative words reflect on our relationships too. Someone on a relationship podcast once said, "You go around saying men are scum. Men are not worth it. Tell me, just how do you expect to meet a man who isn't scum, Who won't hurt you, who won't break your heart, or do all the evil things you think would go wrong in that relationship? As a man, you keep saying all ladies are gold diggers. They all want your money and nothing else, man, you would never find a lady that does not want your money only".

By the words you speak, you're telling the universe without knowing, "I want these things. I want this. I believe this. This is what I want." The universe replies to your demands as you laid them out.

THE POWER OF POSITIVE WORDS

Adopting the 'I can do it' mentality is one thing, saying "I can do it" when faced with a difficulty, now that's on a whole different level entirely. Thinking good thoughts go a long way to heal and grow our mind. Speaking good words go a long way to change the things we see physically around us. It goes as far as changing our approach to life, and it calls good things our way. Positive words when spoken by a person have the ability to rub off on another person who hears when they are spoken.

You wake up feeling blue, and then you walk up to the mirror, look into it, and say "Today is going to be a great day." You're still feeling blue, but a continuous repeat of those words will begin to uplift your mood slowly, and just like that, the universe hears you, and it begins to reply, first in ways you cannot notice. It might be from the little girl that hands you a flower by the sidewalk or the old man that smiles at you or the lady that compliments your looks. The universe is throwing your way beautiful heart touching scenarios that would make you want to smile and cry at the same time. And when you return home at night, you will look back at the day, while you brush your teeth heading for bed, and you will go to bed with a smile on your face. You wake up in the morning in a happier mood than you were the night before, and that will carry you through the day again and again, and all you had to do was simply say, "Today is going to be a great day." They are very simple words. They could easily pass as insignificant, unnecessary, or fickle. But they sent a vibration all around you, touching every positive action you needed to give you a great day, and they brought good things your way. Words!

Telling yourself that you're hardworking, some-how, has the ability to help you manifest that hard work in what you do, it works adversely to telling yourself that you're lazy. It simply brings about a good level of self-motivation. It helps improve the quality of your lifestyle. You cannot go around having a gloomy face every time you tell yourself "I'm happy." It's impossible to produce that kind of contradiction. Someone may have hurt you really bad, and you are angry, and then you begin to speak to yourself, "I'm happy. I'm not mad. I'm at peace." This would help kick you off a bad mood. It might not happen immedi-ately, but it will happen eventually, because while that anger is brewing in your mind, and thoughts of the actions of this person are helping fan the flames, your words of positivity truncate this thought process, and the words begin to immediately reflect on the outside. When you constantly speak happiness to yourself, the law of attraction takes places, and the universe begins to send happiness-generating scenarios your way.

Happy people are generally much more productive. That's a fact.

It also makes you self-aware. You begin to tamper with bad thoughts because you know you should speak positively. And the more positive words you speak, your mind as a routine registers them. The moment you wake up, before you can speak positively about the day, your mind already has it covered.

It reflects on the way you work with people and the way you treat people.

Positive speaking makes you notice and be grateful for all the little things you initially ignored because when the universe sends these beauties down your path, you cannot help but realize just how much they meant and how much change they could make if you had paid more attention to them.

Don't just think about it; speak it! You might be thinking, "I'm fine. I'm fine. I'm okay," and then someone asks, "Hey, how are you?" and the next thing that comes out of your mouth is, "I'm not okay." You just truncated a positive thought with negative words. That's like one step forward and ten more backward. Now you're going to have to start all over again. That's not an impressive pace to grow at. It's not healthy.

Quotes on the power of words

People have since come in terms with the power words possess and have made quotes about them. A few of these quotes are listed below.

1. "Handle them carefully, for words have more power than atom bombs." -Pearl Strachan Hurd

2. "Good words are worth much, and cost little." -George Herbert

3. "No matter what anybody tells you, words and ideas can change the world." -John Keating

4. "The best word shakers were the ones who understood the true power of words. They were the ones who could climb the highest." -Markus Zusak

5. "Whether you think you can or you think you can't, you're right." —Henry Ford

6. "If you look at what you have in life, you'll always have more. If you look at what you don't have in life, you'll never have enough." —Oprah Winfrey

7. "I can't change the direction of the wind, but I can adjust my sails to always reach my destination." —Jimmy Dean

8. "Do or do not. There is no try." —Yoda

9. "Words are free. It's how you use them that may cost you." –KushandWizdom

10. "A simple choice of word can make the difference between someone accepting or denying your message, you can have a very beautiful thing to say, but say it in the wrong words, and it's gone. Words have

power. Words are power. Words could be your power." Mohammed Quahtani [1]

11. "All I need is a sheet of paper and something to write with, and then I can turn the world upside down."[2] -Friedrich Nietzsche

How to use words and their power?

It is not enough to know the negatives and the positives that come with the usage of words. You have to know just how to use the words, and how to tap into the power these words carry. You have to know just how to start making this power begin to manifest in your everyday life.

1. **Ditch the negatives**: 'I cannot do this,' or 'I'm not sure I can make it happen'. Do you say statements like these? Drop them. Replace them with "I can handle this", "I can take care of this", "I can do this", "this would work", and "I am hopeful". Let go of the negatives completely. Don't carry them on with you; they are not healthy.

2. **Stop making absolute statements**: "They are stupid! I cannot work with this". Wrong. Instead use: "They don't seem to

understand, let me teach them" See? That's a lot better. It will make them more receptive to learning because it has made you more open to teaching.

3. ***No more apologies***: "I'm sorry but..." No! Do you have something to say? Say it! Stop apologizing for having an opinion. Give your opinions respectfully and politely, but never ever apologize for them. Doing this waters down the potency of what effect the words were supposed to have. It means you already thought you were wrong, so you apologized beforehand. It means you are not even confident in the fact that you have an opinion. Stop apologizing.

4. **'Do', don't 'try to'**: Stop saying you'd try to do certain things. Say you would do them instead. You're asked, "Hey can you handle this project?" And you reply with, " I can try to do..." At this point, what you have succeeded in doing is telling the person about to hand you that project, that there is a huge chance you will ruin it. And no matter how badly you wanted that project, it will not be handed to you. Trust has been successfully ruined already. Stop saying

you can try, and start saying you can do. Stop saying you will try, and start saying you will do. Get rid of the word try from your personal list of vocabularies. You can do without it.

5. *Switch the labels*: Quit labeling yourself with negative words. You're not a failure, you're not a lazy person, you're not ugly, you're not worthless, take all those awful labels, light a match to them, and burn them all up. Stop with the self-loathing and negative labeling. Change them up. Use words like I'm beautiful, I'm successful, I'm smart, I'm a star, I'm the best, I'm super, I'm flawless. Each of these positive labels has a way of showcasing themselves eventually on you. And soon, everyone would see you for the new labels you've attracted to yourself.

6. *See problems as opportunities*: Instead of saying, "This is a huge problem", say, "This is an interesting challenge that could be handled". See? You've changed the narrative. Stop seeing them as problems; see them as hurdles that you could just jump over.

7. **Write out inspirational quotes**, pin them somewhere, and read them out always: This should be easy. Find quotes that would be uplifting, write them out, and place them on places where you can find them easily such as your car, bedpost, bathroom mirror, or fridge, just anywhere you know you'd always see them. Activate a quote application on your phone to send them at certain times of the day.

Here are a few inspirational quotes you could look at:

- Nothing is impossible, the word itself says, "I'm possible"! —Audrey Hepburn
- The most common way people give up their power is by thinking they don't have any. —Alice Walker
- If you hear a voice within you say, "You cannot paint, then by all means paint, and that voice will be silenced. —Vincent Van Gogh

Get a sheet of paper, write down these words, and paste them somewhere you can see them every day.

Let them inspire you every day. Read them out! Shout them aloud in your privacy, speak them into your everything, let the universe be disturbed for your sake, tell it you can take on life and its challenges. Speak! Let the words fall out!

We live in a yes-based universe, which answers when we ask with the words we constantly speak out. And when we ask, it answers. It may take time, but the universe sure answers. This begs the question, what are you asking?

Your words are powerful, and how you intend to use them, matter.

You create your own reality, and you create your world. Thus, what you say goes in your universe. Speak that word containing that power into your world, recreate your universe, and send positive vibrations into your atmosphere. Words are powerful, speak!

CHAPTER 9

PRACTICAL WAYS TO INTEGRATE THE LAW OF ATTRACTION INTO YOUR DAILY LIFE

" It's unlimited what the universe can bring when you understand the great secret that thoughts become things."

As humans, we have the capacity to create and, at the same time, destroy. When you hear someone invented something, that person has decided to use his own capacity to create. Our capacity to create and achieve great success starts from the mind. The mind is very powerful. You could create or destroy with it, and this is what brings about the law of attraction. Have you ever wondered why each time you woke up cranky and annoyed, that day is always filled with so many uninteresting events and, in some cases, it can lead to a bad day, but if you wake up excited and happy, you will have a productive day? Jack Canfield defines it as, "The law of attraction states that whatever you focus on, think about, read about, and talk about intensely, you're going to attract more of into your life."

Do not allow circumstances or situations to ruin your day. Someone can piss you off, and you choose to dwell on that offense. If you do that, there is a high chance that the rest of your day will be so terrible, and everyone will turn you off. That is how the law of attraction works.

According to the principles of the law of attraction, it is advised that you should be prepared to receive. It is your job to be in a position that is ready to receive. For example, if your dream is to be a medical doctor, you prepare by going to medical school and study, or you want to be a musician, learn to play a musical instrument and listen to other musicians you aspire to be like. If you act as you have it, then it will soon be yours. Like Paulo Coelho said in his book "The Alchemist," "When you want something, all the universe conspires in helping you achieve it". When you are determined to have something, it is the job of the universe to align and create opportunities to help you have it.

The law of attraction is not some form of magic that simply happens because the brain pays more attention and preferentially stores and scan negative events. You need to consciously and continually build positive mental muscle. That is why, as humans, it is easier for us to forget how good someone has been in the past, but we will definitely remember the bad things they have done even if it is just once. Everyone has some negative patterns that have been formed over time in our minds. They are layers of stories, limiting beliefs, and fear that has picked its root deep in our minds. It cannot be replaced in one day by thinking positively, but the good news is that it can be worked on.

In order to erase these thoughts and master the law of attraction positively, you have to undo these patterns that have been registered unconsciously by replacing them with positive and empowering patterns. This is more like saying there is a need to rewire the brain. It may sound so difficult, but it is not actually. The magic is not in big things; it is in consistency! By implanting positive daily practices and then practicing them, you will gradually master the act and function from a place of calmness, and these acts will become habits that help to shape your thought patterns. Don't be in a hurry about them, but with time, you will master the routine, and it will become a part of you and with time, you overcome every negative belief.

Here are some of the daily practices you can implement that can help you attract success:

1. ***Pay attention to what you focus on***: The first thing to pay serious attention to is what you focus on. Pay attention to what is going on right and what is wrong. This will help you to narrow down your thoughts. While trying to achieve your goals and dreams, you will come across challenges and obstacles, but when you choose to focus on what is right, you become a problem solver, and you have positive energy to achieve even more. Stop paying attention to all the wrong things, but focus on those things that are going on well.

2. ***Write down your worries***: Because the brain pays a lot of attention to negative things, it is natural for you to get worked up and worried all the time. Keep a worry

list for the minimum of three weeks. Each time you have to worry about something, just write it down. This will help you release the heavy energy that got you stuck and not just that, by the time you are going back to your list at the end of the three weeks, you will realize that a lot of the things you were worried about were not even worth the stress. With this action, your brain will come to understand that worry is a waste of energy.

3. ***Practice diaphragmatic breathing:*** Diaphragmatic breathing is also called deep breathing. This breathing is done and achieved by contrasting the diaphragm, the belly expands while performing this exercise but the chest does not rise. Every morning, breathe from the belly and not the chest. This is the best way to achieve the diaphragmatic breathing. This breathing activates the parasympathetic nervous system. It helps you to relax and breathe. This breathing helps to produce a sense of calmness and relaxation while taking inspired and productive action.

4. *Quiet your worries and agitation by meditating*: Meditation has the power to quiet down your worries and monkey mind (the monkey mind means being unsettled and restless). Meditation does not mean that you stop thinking. It only helps you to grip your thoughts and soften them. Meditation helps you to keep your eyes off every stressful and negative pattern you have formed over time.

5. *Move your body and feel good*: Negative emotions get stored up in the body on a cellular level, and moving is one major way to relieve yourself of stress and get rid of negative energy. It does not have to be so tedious and intense. It could be as simple as dancing, exercise, walking, or Yoga.

6. *Keep a gratitude journal*: Gratitude is one of the ways to activate positive energy. Each time you are grateful, you are simply asking for more, and it has a way of raising your positive vibration. When you realize your fortune and appreciate your blessings, you know you are in for a big ride. Don't let a day pass without you filling your

gratitude journal. It could be as simple as the stranger that paid your transport fare on the bus, and by the time you look back at the end of the week, you will realize you have achieved a lot.

7. **Write your goals down**: It is not enough to know your goals. There is a need to write them down. Writing them down will give you a clearer picture, and it will also bring about inspired actions to achieve them. When you come up with actions, it fuels you to achieve them, you connect to the feeling of having your goals achieved, and this connection gives you positive energy and vibrations. These vibrations act as magnets to attract people, circumstances, etc. that will help you achieve your goals. Don't just write it down. Place it around your house especially in your bedroom, so you see it every day.

8. **Visualize your dreams**: It was John Muir who said, "The power of imagination makes us infinite." When you begin to visualize your dreams, it gives a picture of your future and that feeling alone is

exciting. Read your goals out in the morning, and do the same at night. Then after reading, spend some minutes visualizing them. Spend some time in the subconscious!

9. *Paint your dream like an artist*: After visualizing your dreams, you need to start thinking like an artist who paints on a canvas. Start this process with an empty canvas by clearing your mind. Then you begin to slowly and patiently add fresh things to your canvas. These things are individual elements that will form pieces of your final art. They are the things that you actually want. Then you put yourself on the canvas, and start interacting with the elements you added earlier. You will realize that there are so many possibilities. You can always get a new car, go and continue your education, or get a new job. You will realize that the opportunities are limitless, and you can do anything you want to do. As you create and visualize your art, you will realize that you badly want the dream to be accomplished. Then you get to think of the actions to take to get you there. New

ideas will pop into your mind, and you need to take action. Without action, you only will be a wisher. You need to start seeing yourself do new things that will get to where you want to be.

10. *Feel like you already have what you want*: Be like a little child who has no feeling of 'impossibility.' Every child always believes his parents are the richest. The feelings have a way of attracting what you want. For example, you have been dreaming of buying a particular type of car, feel like you have it already by visiting the car dealer, and go for a test ride or feel like you are a millionaire. You will act and dress like one. What you feel is what you believe.

11. *Speak it like you have it*: What you continuously speak is what you want, and the universe has a way of bringing it your way. When you speak each day what you want, it comes into existence. Start confessing positively, and you will have it.

DAILY TIMER TO HELP YOU WORK WITH THE LAW OF ATTRACTION

How exactly do you integrate all these practices mentioned above so as to enjoy great success by following the law of attraction?

07:00: Imagine and visualize: When you get up in the morning, even if you had nightmares or you had a long night, or like the saying goes if you woke up on the wrong side of the bed, imagine and visualize. Whatever the case may be, you have the power to choose your outcome. Begin your day by visualizing how beautiful your day will be. See yourself smiling into your office and your boss praising you for a job well done. It doesn't have to take a lot of time. In two or five minutes, you should be done.

07:05: Write and focus on your daily goals: After meditating, pick up your journal and write down what you plan to achieve for the day. Take your time to think through, and write down what you will like to do for that day. Nothing is too little as long as it is leading to your major dream and transforming your life. For example, it could be spending an hour reading a book or talking to your boss about your new idea or some minutes learning new things about your field or skill on the internet.

07:35: Declare your positive affirmations: What you say is what you become. As you are getting ready to go to work or school, spend some seconds confessing the affirmations of how you want the day you be. Choose something simple but positive. For example, you could say "Today will end well, and I will be productive", "I am making great success today", or "Today I make enough sales". "Speak what you seek until you see what you've said" (Anonymous).

8:05: Discuss your plans with your friends: While having breakfast with your family or friends, talk about what you plan to achieve (speak with confidence). For example, you could say, "I'm getting my own apartment soon", or "I'm getting a better and well-paying job soon". What you say, you have, so you speak like you have it. Even if they laugh at you, don't get discouraged.

8:35: Random act of Kindness: As you make your way to work or school, challenge yourself to do a simple random act of kindness. Putting a smile on someone's face has a way of giving you positive energy. It will affect your thought pattern and make you feel like a champion. A very simple act could be paying a stranger's transport fare on the bus, giving your seat to another person, or complimenting someone. Just do something that puts a smile on someone's face.

8:45: *Spread positive energy*: As you step into your office, spread positive energy. Smile and greet everyone you come across. Report something positive that happened during the course of the week, explain and encourage others that the week will be great, and be genuinely interested in others. Avoid negative comments and gossips. It could ruin your positive energy.

12:00 *Continue spreading positive energy*: As the day progresses, make sure you continue spreading positive energy. Encourage your colleagues on their progress, inspire others with new ideas, and maintain the positive energy around you.

13:00 – *Be kind to yourself*: You have been kind to others, so it is okay to treat yourself well. During your lunch hours, be kind to yourself. Treat yourself to a healthy and nutritious meal.

18:00 – *Reflect and evaluate your day*: As the day ends and you have dinner with your friends, reflect how your day went. Share the most interesting part of your day with them, and make sure you avoid anything that will bring negative comments. Even if you do not achieve your goals, don't feel bad, and if you are not seeing the result of the law of attraction, don't be hard on yourself. It takes time.

21:00- *Meditate*: When you are about to wind down for the day, find a quiet and peaceful position to meditate. Engage in diaphragmatic breathing, relax your muscles, and let the feeling of peace envelope your mind. While meditating, you will realize that your worries are diminishing. You could also decide to do a little exercise after meditating

22:00 – *Write in your gratitude journal:* Think about the little things you are grateful for, and write them down. Write down things that inspire gratitude. You could even write about your random act of kindness, the smile you put on someone's face, and even something as little as safety could be written down. It is a reason to be grateful.

"Nurture great thoughts, for you will never go higher than your thoughts." Benjamin Disraeli

The law of attraction might be an old philosophical ideology, but it is still very relevant and powerful. This law teaches you how to make your life better and get you fulfilled and satisfied by harnessing your thoughts. By being positive, you attract positive things into your daily life. This law gives us real support and confirmation that "like attracts like". You can make things happen for you when you decide to pay attention to your thought pattern. Your mood and attitude are dependent on your thoughts so the best and easiest way to improve your life is to think positively. Like the words of Mohammed Ali, "If my mind can conceive it, and my heart can believe it, then I can achieve it." It is no wonder Mohammed Ali was a big success because he applied the law of attraction to achieve great productivity. As long as your mind can process it, choose to believe, and then the universe will work it out for you!

CHAPTER 10

FREQUENTLY ASKED QUESTIONS

hat does it mean to have A High Or Low Vibration?

Everybody has their personal vibration, and it changes constantly. Your vibration is the vitality you convey into the universe because of what you think, how you act, the manner in which you feel, and what you accept. In case you're vibrating on a high frequency, you draw in greater, better, and all the more satisfying things from the world. In the interim, in case, you're vibrating on a lower recurrence, you're likely worn out and feeling low, which makes it harder to draw in what you need. There are some simple and ground-breaking strategies for making sense of your present vibration and changing it to suit your motivations.

. . .

To what extent Does It Take to Manifest Something?

Truth be told, the sooner you can develop an attitude of all-inclusive appreciation and inspiration about each passing minute, the almost certain you are to show an undeniably better life at a quicker rate. A lot of people who have effectively utilized the law of attraction note that they can see they showed their desire at correctly the opportune time for them (which is generally not exactly when you'd figure it would be). In spite of the fact that it sounds like a banality, there is a lot to be delighted in about life's journey, and in the event that you can figure out how to do as such, you'll turn out to be progressively good at manifesting.

How Do I Know If I'm Using The Law Of Attraction Properly?

Give your instinct a chance to control you with regard to making a decision about whether you're utilizing the law of attraction in the correct way. In the event that you feel somewhat better each day, you are empowered to see the good side of things much of the time and can see the unmistakable advances you've made in preparation for the life want, at that point you're utilizing the law of attraction adequately. These are signs that you're uplifting your vibration, and you're starting to draw in the things you want.

Is There One Law of Attraction Technique I Need To Use?

There are many activities and systems that you can use to support your indication potential. The most regularly used are visualization, dream boarding, and determinations. In any case, I would urge you to find out about whatever strategies that are expected under the circumstances, and use the ones that promptly spark motivation in you—this is an indication that something in you is reacting to a particular exercise, perceiving its capacity. In addition, you should not hesitate to alter all of these activities to suit your wants and your kind of person. Be lively, and test to your heart's substance.

What moves should I make?

As proposed earlier in the book, after you've enacted thankfulness, dropped a few negatives, and additionally, try to manifest daily. It's quite normal to ponder what to DO after that. That is to say, we need to make a type of move to influence our fantasies to occur, isn't that so? Wise intentional makers realize they don't need to do anything, other than what feels good. If it's not a cheered action, it won't help! So, except if/until you feel a major solid pleasant inclination to accomplish something, skip it. On the off chance that it feels like a should, an expected to, or any kind of exertion or battle, it'll just moderate advancement. Keep in mind that Universe does the "how" – you simply center around the "what." That's the place your actual power lies.

How long does it take?

In such a case that you're working to the perfection of acknowledging life, having a ton of fun and going about as though you've just got what you needed, you wouldn't feel a "void" or fretfulness for something to occur. Realize that asking the question of "when will it happen" removes you from the arrangement that lets your blessing from heaven. Having said that, on the off chance that you've taken the necessary steps to get in line with what you need, you'll see signs or proof of advancement decently soon. A long time at the outside; typically, sooner. In case you're not seeing those signs, it is possible that you're not as aligned as you think you are, or you're simply not seeing things that are occurring. That is a decent time for a mentor or gathering support.

Am I doing it right?

The way to knowing whether what you're drawing in is working is the manner by which you feel. In case you're feeling much improved, you are progressing nicely! It's that basic. On the off chance that you're not feeling good, at that point, it merits exchanging things up. In case you're not feeling more joyful, progressively upbeat, or possibly lighter with some help, the work you're doing is in vain. All things considered, relaxing might be the best answer until further notice.

CHAPTER 11
DAILY AFFIRMATIONS

LOVE AND ROMANCE

1. All of my relationships are long-term and offer a positive, loving experience.
2. I am worthy of love and deserve to receive love in abundance.
3. I love those around me and I love myself. Others show me love.
4. I attract loving and caring people into my life.
5. My partner and I are both happy and in love. Our relationship is joyous.
6. I am thankful for the love in my life and I am thankful for my caring partner.
7. I only attract healthy, loving relationships.

8. I am with the love of my life. We both treat each other with respect.
9. I happily give and receive love each day.
10. I am so thankful for my partner and how caring they are.
11. Each day I am so grateful for how loved I am and how much people care about me.
12. I know and trust that the Universe will only bring me loyal, supporting, and loving relationships.
13. I open my heart to love and know that I deserve it.
14. Wherever I go and whoever I am with, I find love.
15. I deserve to receive the love I get, and I open myself to the love the Universe gives me.
16. I am open to marriage and attracting my future spouse.
17. My love (and/or marriage) grows stronger every day.
18. I am capable and deserving of a long lasting relationship.
19. My relationship will be open, honest, and full of abundance.

20. Love surrounds me and everyone around me.
21. I am attracting my dream future.
22. I am confident, self-assured, and full of charisma.
23. My partner is a reflection of me.
24. I will never give up on finding true love.
25. I exhale negativity and inhale happiness.
26. Today, I will continue to create the foundation of a happy and loving relationship.
27. I love my soulmate and I love myself.
28. A happy partnership is supportive, balanced, and affectionate.
29. I am manifesting my dream partner.
30. The law of attraction is a natural law that attracts what we focus on into our lives. Today, I will attract love and happiness.
31. My relationships are always fulfilling.
32. I love being in a relationship.
33. Happiness begins with me and me alone. I have the power to create my own happiness.
34. I let go of my past relationships and look to the future.
35. I only think positively about love.

MONEY

1. I am attractive to money and prosperity. Success is drawn to me.

2. I love money. Money is important.

3. I can make money easily.

4. There's no limit to the amount of money I can make.

5. I receive all the wealth and abundance I deserve.

6. I live a successful, abundant, and fulfilled life.

7. I embrace new avenues of making money.

8. I cut out all negative energy relating to money.

9. I welcome an unlimited source of money.

10. I use the money to improve my life and the life of others.

11. My actions lead to constant prosperity.

12. My finances surpass my dreams.

13. I am in charge of my wealth.

14. Money works for me. It is my servant.

15. I am at peace with having huge amounts of money

16. Money has a positive impact on my life.

17. I can gracefully cope with huge success.

18. Money gives me joy and comfort.

19. Having huge amounts of money does not affect my spirituality.

20. I can make money and still fall in love.

21. I am so happy and grateful that money flows to me easily and effortlessly.

22. My relationship with money gets better and better every day.

23. I release all resistance to receiving money.

24. I love attracting money.

25. Isn't it wonderful that I constantly attract opportunities to receive more money?

26. I have more money than I could ever spend.

27. I am worthy of money.

28. Money falls into my lap in miraculous ways.

29. I have millions of dollars in multiple bank accounts.

30. My money allows me to have a life I love.

31. People love giving me money.

32. I naturally attract money.

33. I enjoy the money.

34. I have fun earning money.

35. It is safe to be wealthy.

36. I love how easily I manifest money.

37. I am happy, healthy, and wealthy.

38. I can easily afford anything I want.

39. I am a good money manager.

40. I trust that more money is coming to me.

41. Every dollar I spend comes back to me

multiplied.

42. I trust money.

43. I love having multiple streams of income.

44. I am worthy of money.

45. I deserve to be financially rewarded.

46. My income is constantly increasing.

47. I am grateful for the money I already have and the money that's on its way to me now.

48. It's easy to make money.

49. It's safe for me to have more than enough money.

50. It's safe for me to release what isn't working.

51. It's easy for me to change my money story.

52. I release my resistance to money.

53. I reclaim my money power.

54. I am what a wealthy person looks like.

55. There is room for me at the top.

56. I make empowered financial decisions.

57. I am aligned with the energy of wealth and abundance.

HEALTH

1. I am worthy of good health.

2. I am open to seeing everything that is no longer serving me, and I am willing to see it all with love.

3. I fully accept where I am and am ready to seize this opportunity to grow.

4. I focus on positive progress.

5. I am supported and loved in this healing journey of mine.

6. I create good health by talking and thinking about my wellness.

7. I most love the parts of me that need love the most right now.

8. Even though there is discomfort inside of me, I love and approve of myself.

9. I am in control of the mental atmosphere I create. Thoughts can be changed and the positive thoughts I choose are helping me heal.

10. I am free to be new at this moment.

11. I release all negativity because it's not who I am. I make way for love because that's who I really am.

12. I am a friend to my body. I forgive my body and treat it with the same loving kindness I would like to receive.

13. No matter what has been or will be, my inner light can't be extinguished.

14. I treat my discomfort and pain like I would an innocent child. I tend to my body with unconditional compassion and care.

15. I am doing everything I can to help my body be

well as quickly as possible.

16. I choose thoughts that create a healthy atmosphere within and around me.

17. I am a willing participant in my own wellness plan.

18. I am open to new ways of improving my health.

19. Every choice I make, I make it with mindfulness and a love of life. Whatever it is that I do, I love myself through it.

20. I am a survivor.

21. My body knows how to heal itself. I allow the intelligence of my body to move my health forward.

22. I am on the path of expansion, always learning. I respect the process even when I do not understand it.

23. I am so grateful to be alive. I cherish being here.

24. I am willing to be with all of my thoughts and feelings without admonishing them. Instead of turning away, I stay and understand.

25. I am looking for ways to express love. I am looking for beauty in the present moment. I am looking for beacons of hope everywhere I go.

HAPPINESS

1. I am receiving abundance now in expected and unexpected ways.

2. I am increasingly confident in my ability to create the life I desire.

3. I am acting on inspiration and insights and I trust my inner guidance.

4. I am giving and receiving all that is good and all that I desire.

5. I am receiving infinite, inexhaustible and immediate abundance.

6. I am creating my life according to my dominant beliefs; and I am improving the quality of those beliefs.

7. I am constantly striving to raise my vibration through good thoughts, words, and actions.

8. I am making a meaningful contribution to the world, and I am wonderfully compensated for my contribution.

9. I am willing to believe that I am the creator of my life experience.

10. I am willing to believe that by raising my vibration, I will attract more of what I desire.

11. I am willing to believe that by focusing on feeling good, I make better choices that lead to desired results.

12. I am worthy of love, abundance, success, happiness, and fulfillment.

CHAPTER 12
REFERENCES

Anon, (n.d.). [online] Available at: https://www.thedailymind.com/happiness/14-quotes-about-getting-and-staying-happy/, n.d [Accessed 20 Feb. 2019].http://gosforthcent.newcastle.sch.uk/wordsmiths/

Economy, P. (2015). *26 Brilliant Quotes on the Super Power of Words.* [online] Inc.com. Available at: https://www. Inc.com/peter-economy/26-brilliant-quotes-on-the-super-power-of-words.html [Accessed 20 Feb. 2019].

AwakenTheGreatnessWithin. (n.d.). *35 Inspirational Quotes On The Law Of Attraction | AwakenThe-GreatnessWithin.* [online] Available at:

https://awakenthegreatnesswithin.com/35-inspirational-quotes-law-attraction/ [Accessed 20 Feb. 2019]

Hurst, K. (n.d.). *35 Positive Affirmations For Love, Romance And Marriage*. [online] The Law Of Attraction. Available at: http://www.thelawofattraction.com/affirmations-love-romance/ [Accessed 20 Feb. 2019].

Daniel, E. (n.d.). *37 Money Affirmations to Change Your Life - Apply the Law of Attraction*. [online] Apply the Law of Attraction. Available at: https://www.applythelawofattraction.com/money-affirmations/ [Accessed 20 Feb. 2019]

Mindvalley Blog. (2017). *12 Life-Changing Law of Attraction Affirmations - Mindvalley Blog*. [online] Available at: https://blog.mindvalley.com/law-of-attraction-affirmations/?utm_source=google [Accessed 20 Feb. 2019]. 2017

Gwatkin, J. (2015). *The Ancient Origins of The Law of Attraction. – Unveiling Knowledge*. [online] Unveiling-knowledge.com. Available at: http://www.unveiling-knowledge.com/the-ancient-origins-of-the-law-of-attraction/ [Accessed 20 Feb. 2019].

AFTERWORD

"The law of attraction states that whatever you focus on, think about intensely, read about, and talk about intensely, you're going to attract more of into your life." – Jack Canfield [1]

It's surprising to say but the truth is that some people haven't even heard of the law of attraction, but use it from time to time unknowingly. It is believed that we, as humans, are governed by laws which when followed will be very prosperous. It is no news that the law of attraction is one secret to getting everything you've ever wanted in life. Sometimes in life, we need to do things deliberately in order to get it done. Consciously focusing your mind and attitude into bringing something that you really want into reality is very necessary. The law of attraction is a very relevant factor in the world because it makes us believe that whenever we put a key focus on what we want to achieve, it comes to pass. Clearly, having sad and discouraging thoughts constantly will attract sad and discouraging things to you and having positive and encouraging thoughts will attract positive things to you.

Living by this law might seem easy to do, but it isn't really because we tend to get carried away with the struggles we have, and forget that focusing on previous disappointments will most definitely not bring any positivity. This is the main reason why we need to deliberately follow this law of attraction to guide us from attracting negativity to ourselves. Apart from knowing what the law of attraction is, there are other things we need to be familiar with this to make it work for us effectively. We will be looking at a key component in the law of attraction, how it can guide you, what this law can do for you, and how to use the law of attraction effectively.

Knowing the key component of anything will enable you to take 'the bull by the horn' and get things done. In this case, a key component of the law of attraction is the mind. The mind has a lot to do with this law and understanding its ability will enable you to know how to use the law of attraction effectively.

The mind is a key component in all human beings and understanding how the mind works will benefit you greatly. One major fact about the mind is that information that goes into it was permitted by you. The mind is very powerful, and we need to guide it because it can also be easily contaminated. The truth about the mind is that negative things tend to stay in longer, but we will learn how to keep the negatives out. As human beings, we've been opportune to be able to condition our mind however we want but most of us usually don't make use of this opportunity. You have the ability to choose what stays in your subconscious mind and whenever you find out that you are trying to store positive information into your mind but it's just not working, it's because the negative thought is getting the best of you. Then there's one solution to that, which is increasing the frequency. For example, whenever negative thoughts about a particular thing won't go away, you need to speak positive things into your mind frequently, and with this, the negative thought will have no choice but to get out of your mind.

One major fact is that we cannot use thoughts to fight thoughts and which is why we need to speak when necessary. Speaking out positive words like "I'm worth it", "I can do this", "I am not a failure", "money is coming my way", "I am successful", and many more positive things will condition your mind to believe it even if it hasn't happened yet. Another good fact about the mind is that it can't differentiate between what is real and what isn't. With this, we can condition our mind to believe positive things and by doing this, our mind now has the permission to make us work hard enough to bring our wishes into reality. The picture in your head is so beautiful and then coming out of that fantasy and seeing the not so pretty part of your reality will definitely make you want to work hard to turn your fantasy into reality. You own your mind, so anything that you don't want to be in it can be taken out even if not subconsciously but consciously.

THE LAW OF ATTRACTION AS A GUIDE

"Think the thought until you believe it, and once you believe it, it is." – Abraham Hicks

Using the law of attraction as a guide in your life will only make it smooth and amazing. Knowing that the law of attraction puts negative thoughts with negative results should motivate you to consciously push out the negatives and exalt the positives. Apart from our thoughts, other factors that are also involved with the law of attraction are our emotions, feelings, and desires.

Our emotions come as a result of circumstances or experiences. Normally, a sad situation isn't expected to make you happy, it's meant to make you sad. Exciting events can't make you sad, they make you excited and that's how it has always been. Now, working with the law of attraction, sad events shouldn't make you sad, they should encourage you. As it was mentioned earlier, the negative things tend to stay longer than the positives and this is because we allow ourselves to be tormented by negative circumstances forgetting that it doesn't last at least if we don't want it to. A person can be sad for two months and be happy for just a few hours. Allowing negative emotions to stay longer than it's supposed to will only get the best of us. If we can learn to accept the fact that sad times are not supposed to be permanent, we will be doing a lot better.

When sad emotions are just all over the place, inevitably our thoughts will be negative because our mind has been clouded by negativity, and focusing on the negatives will only attract more negative things. This is because, whenever we are sad, we just make ourselves believe that nothing good is about to happen or that we are so unlucky. You need to get a hold of your emotions and know that it's only for a while. It's not like you're not allowed to be sad but don't give it enough time to put dark clouds around your mind. Be upset but also be willing to shake it off quickly. As long as it didn't kill you, it can only make you stronger!

Our desires have a very important role to play in the law of attraction. As a person, the desire to be rich, happy, motivated, love, money, and in time, it'll come to you. There is nothing in this world we can't get if we put our mind to it. Your biggest limitation is your mind! Do not be scared or timid to imagine great things, because everything is possible. Having big dreams and aspirations are the first things that motivate us to work hard. Desiring the small or basic things of the worlds will bring you those. Every great person in the world has one head, one nose, two ears, and well, everything a normal human is meant to have.

Feelings come and go sometimes without our consent. Feelings in relation to the law of attraction should not be changing anyhow. Mood swing is not a friend to the law of attraction because it comes with happy moods sometimes and sad moods other times mostly for no reason. You need to consciously take charge of your feelings because, for example, when you're feeling down, you don't expect innovative thoughts to come to you, and it'll just be sad and depressing thoughts. You can't allow your life to go bad just because you're not feeling happy. Work hard to get rid of mood swings so that the negative moods won't inevitably attract negative things to you.

When the law of attraction becomes a guide for your life, you begin to notice positive changes and improvement. As time goes on, you subconsciously find yourself in positive environments always and around positive people. You will hardly find yourself feeling depressed or down for even the most legitimate reasons.

What you can expect after practicing the law of attraction

"Thoughts become things. If you see it in your mind, you will hold it in your hand." – Bob Proctor [1]

1. *You see the best in everything*: The law of attraction makes you hope for the best in life and by always hoping for the best, you tend to see the bright side of everything. When you allow the law of attraction to guide you, your life becomes easier. It's not like you won't have challenges because you will but you'll see them as challenges and

not problems because every challenge that comes your way can be conquered by you alone. Saying you have problems make it harder to want to overcome them, but tagging it as a challenge makes you want to overcome it and get stronger. Seeing the best in everything will always bring the best of everything to you.

2. *You feel constantly encouraged:* Following the law of attraction, you get encouraged even everything around you is discouraging. Just because you don't want to attract negative things your way, you won't let yourself get discouraged. Even when people see the worst in a situation, you don't, because you know you can overcome it. It becomes your wingman, always there to hype you.

3. *Good people are attracted to you:* The law of attractions links positive thoughts, desires, feelings, and emotions to positive outcomes. If you keep desiring a person to love you, for example, all your thoughts, your feelings, and your focus are on finding a good person to love, inevitable that person finds you. Apart from love, desiring

a person that will mentor you or that will be able to always be there to aid your financial needs will come to you because you first created the thought and interest in your mind, and so the law of attraction brought it to life.

4. ***You become hardworking:*** One fact about following the law of attraction is that it makes you want the best things, and it also makes you willing and able to work for them. Creating that perfect picture in your head is the first motivation to wanting to achieve it. For example, fantasizing about getting a good job and then waking up to see that you are jobless and unfulfilled will push you to willingly do what you need to do to get that dream job. You keep seeing that dream, and you keep trying to bring it to reality.

5. ***You attract the best things In Life:*** When you allow the law of attraction to guide you, you notice that the best things in life begin to locate you because you concentrate on them and work hard to achieve them. Even if you have some setbacks, the fact that you believe it's only

for a moment works for you by compensating you with something better. No person is meant to live with negativity because it's just very unrewarding. A lot of people that say negative things, thing negative things, and don't desire big things love the use the word 'unlucky' and the truth is that it does not exist. As long as you believe that you are unlucky, unlucky things will keep happening to you. Set your mind to believe that you are favored and privileged and it'll work for you. Whatever you believe in will work for you, and that is a fact. Believe in positivity completely, and it'll work for you.

How To Use The Law Of Attraction Effectively?

When we talk about making the law of attraction very effective, there are two major things that we need to focus on. They are how frequently you speak and think about the positive things you want and the work you put into bringing it to pass.

When you want something that seems too big or too great to achieve, it's understandable if you feel a little discouraged about it coming to pass. To tackle this hint of disbelief, you need to keep thinking about it and to keep speaking it as much as possible and by doing this; you slowly start to believe it. Focusing your energy into what you want to achieve will make you believe it can happen because if you don't believe that it can happen then it won't. Sometimes, our dreams might seem too big to achieve, and so the first step to making the law of attraction a reality is to first believe it yourself and how do you do that? By focusing all your attention to that dream!

Secondly, to make the law of attraction work for you, you need to be willing to put in the work. As soon as you believe in what you want to achieve completely, automatically, you will be willing to work for it. Dreams are sweet but the fact is that you will wake up from them. Don't waste your dreams by just staying home and wishing. Use that vision as a motivation to start and finish. One fact about humans is that we usually do put value in what we don't work hard for. Imagine that as you wish for money it appears, you would spend it on useless things because you did not work for it. Working hard to bring your dreams to reality will make you work even harder to remain there. A lazy person has the biggest dreams, but is still the poorest of them all why? Because he isn't wise enough to use those dreams as a motivation to be great.

Working with these two things will make the law of attraction work for you in areas you never imagined. You need to be willing to go all out for what you want and this is possible because you already have a dream that you believe in. You need to deliberately turn your attention to that thing that you want to achieve, and also consciously work hard to get it. The word 'deliberately' is used because it's understandable that you can get distracted by other things or other negative energy so you need to deliberately remind yourself of what you want and the fact that you need to work hard to achieve it.

Techniques You Can Use With The Law Of Attraction

1. Thinking out loud
2. Reading motivational books
3. Watching inspiring movies
4. Taking down notes on what you want to achieve
5. Surrounding yourself with positive people
6. Taking conscious actions to make your dreams a reality
7. Investing in building yourself mentally
8. Staying healthy physically and spiritually

Dream big

One thing that must not be forgotten is the fact that thinking positively can be difficult which is why we need to deliberately condition our mind to think positive and working hard.

P.S.

But before you go, I wanted to ask you for one small favor.

If you enjoyed reading this book, could you please consider posting a review on the platform?

Posting a review is the best and easiest way to support the work of independent authors like me.

It would mean a lot to me to hear from you.

>> Leave a review on Amazon US <<

>> Leave a review on Amazon UK <<

Thank YOU,
Zachariah Albert

NOTES

1. A BRIEF HISTORY OF THE LAW OF ATTRACTION

1. (Quote), (Unveilingknowledge.com), (2015)
2. The Hermetic principles, Unveilingknowledge.com, 2015
3. Unveilingknowledge.com, 2015

4. HAPPINESS AND THE LAW OF ATTRACTION

1. www.dailymind.com,n.d

8. WORDS ARE POWERFUL, SPEAK IT

1. (Quotes 1 to 10), (inc.com), (2016)
2. (Quote 7), (gosforthcent.newcastle.sch.uk), (n.d)

AFTERWORD

1. (Quote), (awakenthegreatnesswithin.com),(n.d)

Made in the USA
Monee, IL
24 February 2024

54045260R00098